COMING HOME

FROM THE
COOKBOOK
COLLECTION OF

Lita Sturzaker

John Burton Race

COMING HOME

Photography by
Pia Tryde

EBURY
PRESS

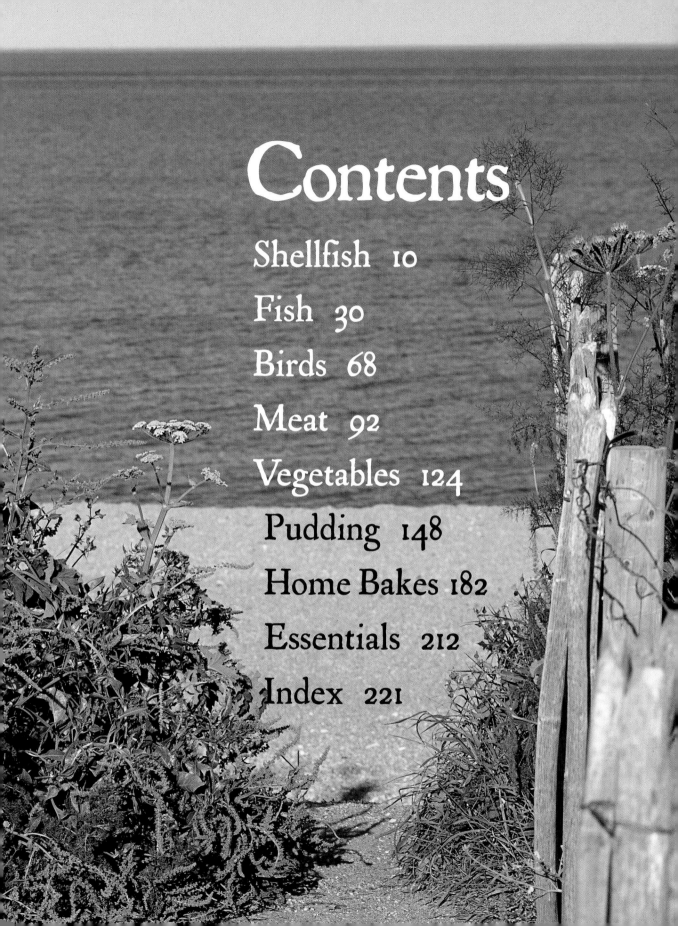

Contents

I like to think that my buying The New Angel was something that was, quite simply, meant to be.

I'd had my first vague thoughts about opening a restaurant in England towards the end of my year's stay in France, while working on *French Leave*. It had been an important year for me in many ways. I had enjoyed living in our farmhouse in the Aude, and introducing my wife, Kim, and six children to a rural way of life that was free from the pressures and strains of our previous existence. More importantly, from a professional point of view, it was an inspirational period in which I went 'back to basics'. Living in that unspoilt area of southwestern France had taught me that food didn't have to be fancy to be good. I rediscovered the pleasures of cooking and eating simple, no-fuss dishes made from seasonal local ingredients – the kind of food that had an honesty I felt I had somehow lost sight of in my years as a Michelin-star chef. By the end of my stay, my excitement and passion for food was greater than ever and, as the time to leave approached, I knew I didn't want to leave those feelings behind. I wondered if it would be possible to capture what I'd learnt and somehow bring it back to England – perhaps by opening a restaurant, though I wasn't sure where.

The plan had always been to return to Oxfordshire, where we had our family home, but we had let it out and, due to complications with the contract, we found that the house wouldn't be vacant for another six weeks. So, when we eventually left the Aude, on that September day in 2003, my feelings of sadness at leaving France were tinged with a sense of frustration and annoyance. But we had to make the best of things, and the children were all in the mood for a holiday, so we drove through France to Spain, and spent a couple of weeks there, then caught the ferry from Santander to Plymouth, where we stayed in rented accommodation for about a month. After pottering around Plymouth for a few days, we decided to explore the general area, and that's when my love affair with Devon, and the area of the South Hams in particular, began.

Everywhere we went, I was struck by the natural beauty of the county – the wide open spaces and green fields that were so reminiscent of France, and the hidden beauty of the old, quintessentially English, sunken lanes with their fantastic hedgerows. Then, gradually, as I drove around, I began to notice the signs of an area rich in natural produce: the iron-rich red soil and lush pastureland that is so perfect for yielding the best meat and dairy produce, the beautiful orchards of apples and pears, the river estuaries with their wonderful range of fresh- and seawater fish and shellfish. There were even vineyards, for heaven's sake. It was France all over again – without the sunflowers. I began to get really excited at the possibilities the region offered, and explored further. It only took a few visits to local producers to make me realise that this wasn't just a wonderful place to have cream teas. Locally reared organic meat, organic fruit and vegetables grown by small-scale producers, a spectacular range of freshly caught fish and seafood, delicious local cheeses . . . the ingredients here were special. After three weeks, I had decided that if I was going to open a restaurant in England, this was the county to do it in, though I still hadn't decided on the town.

All that changed when I went to Dartmouth. One look at that spectacular setting on the River Dart and I was completely bowled over. What a fantastic place, I thought. I couldn't believe we'd always spent our holidays abroad when there was such a lovely slice of England right on our doorstep. There was nowhere else I could possibly consider. But if I bought a restaurant here, there was really only one possible contender: The Carved Angel, once owned by the legendary Joyce Molyneux – to my mind, one of the best British chefs ever. Joyce Molyneux had achieved international fame in the 1960s, producing simple food in accordance with my new-found principles, made from excellent local ingredients, and everything suddenly fell into place. I knew, without a doubt, that buying this lovely waterfront restaurant was the right thing to do. It would be a perfect homecoming. There was just one small snag: it wasn't for sale.

I've never been one to let things like this stand in my way, however, and when we returned to Oxfordshire, I couldn't let it go. I kept coming back down to Devon, determined to try and find a solution. I had decided to make an offer anyway. After endless – often heated – discussions, Kim persuaded me against doing so, and instead to approach the owners about another local restaurant they owned, and which she also liked. We put in an offer for it, though I very much felt that it was second best. The negotiations dragged on, and then, one miserable wet Thursday afternoon in March – call it chance, fate or what you will – we got a phone call from the restaurant owner to say he'd changed his mind and the deal was off. 'Just one thing,' he said, before hanging up, 'I don't suppose you'd be interested in buying The Carved Angel instead . . .?' And that, as they say, was that!

From then on, it was all systems go, both to get the restaurant ready for its reincarnation as The New Angel, and to find somewhere to live. After several failed attempts on my part to find a new home, Kim eventually came down from Oxfordshire and, with her unerring knack in these things, found an old farmhouse in Kingsbridge that everyone loved. And two months of sheer hard work later, on Thursday, 27 May, The New Angel finally opened.

Settling in Devon has been the best homecoming possible. Kim and the children love it here. Olivia, Charles, Amelia and Eliza are all happy in the local schools, while Martha (who didn't want to leave her friends) boards during the week and comes home every weekend. Eve is the only one who was slightly reluctant to move, so I'm afraid I had to resort to some bribery – in the form of a little car and some driving lessons. Now she helps out at the restaurant (along with Olivia) quite happily. Opening The New Angel has been a team effort, which could never have been so easily achieved without the help and support of my family, and the local Devon people. I have been welcomed and made to feel at home everywhere I've gone, for which I am truly grateful. I have also been deeply touched at people's interest in what I've been doing.

I feel more privileged than I can say to have been able to buy The Carved Angel, and to continue its fine traditions of excellence. But although this book is primarily a celebration of the produce of Devon, I also like to think of it as a tribute to the best that Britain, as a whole, has to offer. Some of the dishes included here are from The New Angel repertoire, others are personal or family favourites. But all of them are easy to make, and I hope there's something here for everyone. Most of all, I hope you get as much pleasure from them as I have.

Chapter
I. Shellfish

Finding freshly caught shellfish just over the road was something I'd only ever associated with France ... until Devon. **john**

For me, one of the best things about being in Dartmouth is being so close to the river and sea. Here at The New Angel, we are privileged to have the River Dart virtually on our doorstep and every morning, when I come to work, I never cease to be amazed at the stunning view of Dartmouth harbour that greets me. But the beauty of this location isn't purely aesthetic. For me as a chef – and a great lover of seafood – it's also immensely practical. Due to one of those flawless miracles of Nature, this part of the Dart Estuary is close to the point where the sea flows into the river to produce a magical mingling of waters – and a fantastic range of fresh- and seawater fish and shellfish with a unique flavour.

This is especially true of the local crabs and lobsters, which, caught just offshore, have a subtle sweetness I have rarely found elsewhere. I get endless pleasure from watching the fishermen bring in their catch. In January, it's the cock crabs,

SPECIALITIES

Fish&Chips

COD Haddock Plaice
SKate Lemon Sol

FISH & SEAFOOD
CAUGHT IN THE START BAY

monkfish *Sole*
*Bass *Lemon* *DoverSole*
Brill *Plaice*
*Handpicked Crab *Scallop*

Gammons, Steaks, Chicken, Burger
Vegetarian Dishes
Snacks

The range of seafood in south Devon is fantastic, and I love watching the fishermen bringing in their daily catch. Shellfish, along with fish, is part of everyday life here, and clams, scallops, mussels, lobster and crab, in particular, feature on most local restaurant menus. The last two are my own particular favourites – their meat is delicious, and the shells, finely ground, make a colourful, tasty flavouring for soups.

followed, over the next two months, by the hen crabs, and then, in early spring, my absolute favourite – the lobster catch, brought in right through to May. Coupled with the boats going up and down the river, their line-caught sea bass and mackerel alongside, it's hard to beat. Wonderful!

It's not just crabs and lobsters that this area is renowned for, of course. Mussels, scallops, cockles and clams are all very much in evidence too. At The New Angel, we bring in our scallops from the sea at Beesands, and our mussels from the rivers Dart, Exe and Teign, but the truth is that all this seafood is pretty much available everywhere – even on the beaches. One of our favourite family pastimes is going to Wonwell, a fantastic sandy beach where Eliza and Amelia love collecting the razor-shell clam shells that are washed up on the shore.

Sadly, however, when it comes to enjoying shellfish as a family, that's the closest it gets. Kim has an allergy to all forms of fish and shellfish, and none of the children like eating it, though Eliza likes crab salad and Amelia will try anything – once. All very irritating because, as far as I'm concerned, there are few finer things in life than eating seafood that has been freshly caught, cooked and brought straight to the table.

Mussel Soup

I like to serve this with garlic bread and a large glass of cold German lager.

Serves 6

2 kg mussels

125 g leeks, washed

½ bulb fennel, trimmed

100 g celery, trimmed

60 ml olive oil

80 g unsalted butter

150 g onions, peeled and finely
   chopped

½ bottle of dry white wine

2 garlic cloves, peeled and crushed

1 sprig fresh thyme

1 sprig fresh tarragon

¼ bay leaf

800 ml Fish Stock (see page 214)

270 ml double cream

1 pinch saffron

salt and freshly milled black pepper

juice of ¼ lemon

1. Very carefully clean and scrape all the mussels, removing any barnacles and beards from the outside of the shells. Wash them thoroughly in cold running water.

2. Cut the leeks, fennel and celery into small dice. Set a large, lidded saucepan on the stove, pour in the olive oil and, when it starts to smoke, quickly add the butter. As soon as the butter has melted but not browned, tip in the chopped vegetables and onions.

3. Pour in the white wine, bring it to the boil to burn off the alcohol, then reduce by half. Add the crushed garlic, thyme, tarragon and bay leaf, then pour in the fish stock. Bring to the boil once again, then tip in the mussels and, with a wooden spoon, carefully stir them into the liquid, working from the bottom of the pan to the top. Cover with the lid and cook over a high heat for 8 minutes.

4. When the mussels are cooked they will open up. Turn them out into a colander with a saucepan underneath to catch the juices, discarding any that are not opened. Shake off all the liquid from the mussels and turn them out onto a tray. Scoop the mussels out of their shells and divide them between six soup bowls, reserving a few mussels in their shells for garnishing.

5. Strain the cooking juices through a muslin cloth into another saucepan and bring to the boil, skimming off all the surfacing scum and foam with a ladle. Pour in the cream and bring the soup back to the boil to reduce to a thicker consistency. Add the saffron, season with salt and pepper and pour in the lemon juice. Ladle the soup over the mussels and serve immediately.

Mussel Fritters with Tartare Sauce

This is a good dish for a dinner party because you can cook the mussels in advance, remove them from their shells and, once the batter is ready, putting everything together takes only minutes.

Serves 4 as a main course

1 kg fresh mussels

50 g unsalted butter

1 shallot, diced

250 ml white wine

sea salt and freshly milled black
   pepper

125 g plain flour

30 g cornflour

150 ml lager

150 ml carbonated water

groundnut oil, for deep frying

50 g salad leaves

4 tablespoons Tarragon Vinaigrette
   (see page 219)

4 tablespoons Tartare Sauce
   (see page 217)

Variation

This recipe will work for most shellfish, such as raw langoustine tails, prawns and oysters.

1. Wash and scrub the mussels thoroughly and remove the beards and any barnacles attached to the shells. Tap any open shells on the work surface and discard the ones that refuse to close.

2. Melt the butter in a large shallow lidded pan on the stove, add the shallots and cook for 1 minute. Pour in the wine, bring to the boil, then add some pepper. Tip the cleaned mussels into the pan and cover with the lid. Cook for about 5 minutes, turning the mussels once, stirring from the bottom to the top, then drain them through a colander set over a bowl to catch the stock and put to one side. When the mussels are cool enough to handle, remove them from their shells and dry thoroughly on kitchen paper.

3. Sift the flour and cornflour into a bowl and add some salt and pepper. Add the lager and carbonated water and whisk until you have a thick but smooth batter. Dust the mussels with a little flour.

4. Heat the oil in a large pan or deep-fat fryer until it reaches a temperature of 190°C/375°F. If using a pan, make sure that it is no more than one third full.

5. Coat the mussels, a few at a time, in the batter and fry quickly for about 1 minute. Drain on kitchen paper and keep warm.

6. Toss the salad in the tarragon vinaigrette and arrange in the centre of four large plates. Spoon the mussels around the salad and serve the tartare sauce on the side.

Mussels in Scrumpy Jack

This is a variation of the classic French dish Moules Marinières. In Devon, several restaurants serve the mussels this way, using a dry cider instead of white wine. This recipe also has the addition of apple in the broth, with cream to finish. When in Devon, do as the Devonians do!

Serves 8

3 kg mussels

50 g unsalted butter

1 onion, peeled and finely chopped

2 garlic cloves, peeled and finely chopped

1 stick celery, chopped

1 apple, peeled, cored and chopped

1 sprig thyme

1 bay leaf

300 ml dry Scrumpy Jack or any dry cider

150 ml double cream

salt and coarsely ground black pepper

2 tablespoons finely chopped parsley

Variation

To make Moules Marinières, substitute dry white wine for the cider and leave out the apple.

1. Wash and scrape the mussels and remove the beards (as in the previous recipe). Melt the butter in a large, lidded saucepan and add all the chopped ingredients. Cook for about 5 minutes, stirring occasionally, then add the thyme and bay leaf.

2. Turn the heat up high, pour in the cider and bring to the boil. Next tip in the mussels, stirring them into the liquid with a wooden spoon, working from the bottom of the pan to top, cover with the lid and cook for about 3 minutes until the mussels open.

3. Shake the pan, remove the lid, add the cream and stir into the mixture. Season with a little salt and lots of black pepper, then sprinkle in the chopped parsley.

4. Using a ladle, divide the mussels between eight bowls. Pour some of the broth over them and serve immediately with some crusty white bread.

Crab Soup

I have used spider crab in this recipe, but velvet crab works just as well. There is no need to use a big fleshy crab for this dish – the meat would be wasted and is far better kept for other recipes. One way of killing the crabs is to use the point of a sharp knife and cut straight through into the air vent. However, it is probably more humane to put them in the freezer for a couple of hours.

Serves 8

2 kg fresh live crab
100 ml olive oil
50 g unsalted butter
1 onion, peeled and diced
1 carrot, peeled and diced
2 sticks celery, chopped
1 leek, washed and chopped
½ bulb fennel, chopped
1 bay leaf
1 sprig fresh thyme
1 sprig fresh tarragon
4 garlic cloves, peeled and crushed
150 g tomato purée
4 tomatoes, quartered and deseeded
4 tablespoons Cognac
200 ml dry white wine
2 litres Fish Stock (see page 214)
salt
juice of ½ lemon
125 ml double cream
1 bunch chives (about 20 g), finely
    chopped
cayenne pepper

1. Pull off the top shell of the crab, remove the gills and grit sac, and discard. Pull off the legs and crack the claws, then set aside. With a large knife, chop the crab into manageable-sized pieces.

2. Set a large saucepan on the stove, pour in the olive oil and, as soon as it starts to smoke, add the butter together with the crab pieces. Fry the crab pieces, turning them over with a spoon from time to time for about 10 minutes, until they are browned.

3. Tip in all the chopped vegetables, followed by the herbs and garlic, and stir occasionally. Stir in the tomato purée and add the tomatoes.

4. Flambé the crab with the Cognac and pour in the dry white wine. Bring the wine to the boil, then add the fish stock. Return to the boil, skimming off all the surfacing oil and scum, then turn down the heat and allow the soup to simmer for about 1 hour.

5. Chop the remaining crab legs and claws and, in a food processor, break them up as small as possible. Add to the simmering soup and continue cooking for another 30 minutes.

6. When the soup is cooked, strain it through a colander into another saucepan. Force as much of the liquid as you can from the shells with a wooden spoon. Bring the soup back to the boil and remove all of the surfacing scum, then turn down the heat a little and reduce the soup to thicken.

7. Strain the soup through a fine sieve into another pan, then taste for seasoning – it may need a little salt. Add the lemon juice and ladle the soup into bowls. Float a large dessertspoon of whipped cream on top of each, sprinkle some chives over the cream and a pinch of cayenne pepper. Serve immediately.

Spicy Crab Cakes

I serve these as a starter on my lunchtime menus at The New Angel. It's a good way of using up leftover cooked crab. Make sure there is no shell in the white crab meat.

Serves 4 as a starter

400 g white crab meat

80 g brown crab meat

30 g fresh ginger, peeled and chopped

4 spring onions, finely sliced

zest of 1 lemon

1 sprig coriander, chopped

4 teaspoons Worcestershire sauce

4 dessertspoons Mayonnaise
   (see page 218)

2 eggs

50 g fresh white breadcrumbs

salt and freshly milled black pepper

50 g plain flour

3 tablespoons groundnut oil

100 g mixed salad leaves

2 dessertspoons Tarragon Vinaigrette
   (see page 219)

1. Put a pan of water on the stove to boil and blanch the ginger for 5 minutes. Strain and put to one side.

2. Put the white and dark crab meat, the spring onions, lemon zest, coriander, blanched ginger, Worcestershire sauce and mayonnaise in a large bowl and mix together. Beat one of the eggs and add enough to the mixture to bind it together. Add a few breadcrumbs if it seems too wet, and taste for seasoning. Divide and shape the mixture into four even-sized cakes, place on a tray lined with greaseproof paper or baking parchment, and put in the freezer to harden for 30 minutes.

3. Beat the remaining egg. Lay out three separate bowls on the work surface containing the egg wash, flour and breadcrumbs. Remove the crab cakes from the freezer and, one by one, roll them in the flour, tapping off any excess, then dip them in the egg and finally the breadcrumbs.

4. Heat a large shallow pan on the stove over a medium heat and add the groundnut oil. As soon as the oil starts to smoke, carefully place the crab cakes in the pan. Allow them to brown on one side; this will take about 4 minutes. Turn them over and cook for a further 4 minutes. It is important to make sure that they are hot in the middle. Serve immediately with the mixed leaves bound in the tarragon vinaigrette.

Dartmouth Crab Salad

The crab boats pull up alongside the New Angel so I can take my pick!

Serves 4

500 ml Court Bouillon or Poaching
    Stock (see page 215)
1 large live crab (1–1.2 kg, preferably
    a 'cock' or male crab as these have
    more meat and are easier to clean
    than 'hen' crabs)
100 ml Mayonnaise (see page 218)
2 teaspoons tomato ketchup
a few drops Worcestershire sauce
2 teaspoons Cognac
a few drops of Tabasco
juice of ½ lemon
1 avocado
1 Granny Smith apple, peeled and
    finely chopped
1 shallot, finely chopped
1 pink grapefruit, peeled and
    segmented
2 tablespoons Tarragon Vinaigrette
    (see page 219)
10 cherry tomatoes
1 teaspoon mild curry powder
salt and freshly milled black pepper

1. Bring the court bouillon to the boil in a large saucepan. Put the crab in and boil for 20 minutes.

2. Take the pan off the stove. Remove and cool the crab. Pull off the claws and legs. Carefully crack them open and remove the white meat, trying not to allow any shell to fall into the meat. Set aside.

3. Turn the crab over onto its shell and pull the middle back to expose the inside. Discard the gills or 'dead man's fingers', and scrape all the dark meat into a bowl, then set aside.

4. Mix the mayonnaise and tomato ketchup in a bowl. Add the Worcestershire sauce, 1 teaspoon Cognac and Tabasco. Stir together, add the lemon juice and place in the refrigerator.

5. Halve the avocado and discard the stone. Cut each half into two and peel carefully. Cut each quarter into fine slices and place them in a bowl.

6. Add 1 tablespoon of the tarragon vinaigrette and turn the avocado pieces over with a spoon. Add the apple and shallot and stir together. Set aside.

7. Lay out six large plates. Place a 5 x 6 cm ring mould in the centre of each. Spoon the avocado salad into each mould and press down gently.

8. Take the dark crabmeat and add the remaining teaspoon of cognac. Season with a little salt and lemon juice and spoon it over the avocado.

9. Season the white meat with a little lemon juice. Press it down over the dark meat. Drizzle over a dessertspoon of sauce. Sprinkle over the curry powder.

10. Gently and very carefully remove the moulds. Cut the pink grapefruit segments in half lengthways and arrange them around the base of the crab. Cut the cherry tomatoes in two and place 5 half tomatoes around the outer edge of each plate. Dot the remaining vinaigrette between the tomato halves and serve.

Grilled Langoustines with a Soy Vinaigrette

As with lobsters, langoustines are best split in the raw state while still alive. Most people, however, would find this unpleasant! Cooked langoustines should be cut into two and the entrails removed. Sprinkle with a little olive oil, salt, freshly milled black pepper and lemon juice. Place under a hot grill for 5 minutes and then spoon the soy vinaigrette over them while they are still hot. Grilled langoustine tails work just as well. Serve a light, dry Sauvignon Blanc with this one.

Serves 6

2 kg langoustines

Salad

40 g baby spinach leaves

40 g small rocket leaves

40 g yellow frisée or curly endive

2 shallots, peeled and finely chopped

15 g chives, chopped

salt and coarsely ground black pepper

Soy Vinaigrette

1 garlic clove, peeled and finely chopped

80 ml Tarragon Vinaigrette (see page 219)

1 tablespoon soy sauce

1 tablespoon tamari

juice of ¼ lemon

1. For the salad, wash and thoroughly dry the lettuce leaves, then mix all the ingredients together in a large salad bowl and season the leaves with a little salt and pepper.

2. To make the vinaigrette, place the chopped garlic in a small bowl, and add the cooking juices of the langoustines. Next whisk in the tarragon vinaigrette, soy and tamari sauces, and lemon juice. Stir until fully emulsified and strain the vinaigrette through a fine sieve into a small pan.

3. Warm the vinaigrette on the stove over a gentle heat. Pour half the vinaigrette over the lettuce leaves and mix thoroughly. The remainder can be spooned over the hot grilled langoustines. To serve, place the langoustines in a dish on the table with the bowl of salad, and dig in.

Lobster Salad

This dish is ideal for a summer's lunch, accompanied by a glass of Sharpham's white wine.

Serves 6

6 x 500-g live lobsters (Only use live lobsters. You can freeze the heads and use them later in a fish soup, lobster bisque, lobster sauce or consommé.)

2 litres Fish Stock (see page 214)

40 g fresh tarragon

200 ml Mayonnaise (see page 218)

salt and freshly milled black pepper

12 small new potatoes (about 600 g), scrubbed

3 tablespoons Tarragon Vinaigrette (see page 219)

100 g mixed lettuce leaves (such as yellow frisée, chicory, corn salad and a little rocket)

1 shallot, finely chopped

small bunch chives, chopped

2 tomatoes, blanched, skinned and diced

juice of ¼ lemon

1. Kill the lobsters by inserting the point of a knife quickly into the air vent. Remove the elastic bands around the claws, pull them off, then crack them with a meat bat or heavy metal implement. Be careful during this process just to crack the shell and not to hit the claws so severely that you crush the flesh. Pull off the heads and freeze them for later use. Put the tails and claws in separate bowls and put to one side.

2. Put the fish stock in a large lidded saucepan and bring to the boil. When boiling, add the claws and cook for 5 minutes, then add the tails and cook both for a further 5 minutes. Remove the pan from the stove and carefully strain the contents through a colander set over a bowl. Fill a sink with cold water and put the lobsters in it to cool.

3. Lift the lobsters out of the water and drain. Carefully cut the tail shells and remove the meat. Crack the claws and carefully remove the flesh. Be careful not to rip or break the claws; try to keep them intact. Make a small incision along the middle of the tails and remove the entrail lines, which look like brown thread and run down through the tail of the lobster, and discard. Transfer the lobster meat to a plate and refrigerate until needed.

4. Put a small saucepan half filled with water on the stove to boil. Pick the leaves off the tarragon sprigs and boil for about 3 minutes. Strain through a fine sieve and refresh under cold water. Pat dry with kitchen towel. Chop the tarragon as finely as possible and stir it into the mayonnaise. Refrigerate until needed.

5. Place another pan, half filled with water, on the stove to boil and add a large pinch of salt. When the water boils, add the potatoes and cook for 20 minutes or until tender. Check for doneness by inserting a knife into one of the potatoes – if it falls off, it's cooked. Strain, allow to cool slightly, then, whilst still warm, peel off the skins and cut into slices about 5 mm thick. Put in a bowl, season, and add 1 tablespoon of the tarragon vinaigrette. Set aside.

6. Put the lettuce leaves in a salad bowl. Add the shallot, chives and 1 tablespoon of tarragon vinaigrette and mix together. Set aside.

7. Put the diced tomato in a small bowl. Season with a little salt and milled black pepper and pour in the remaining vinaigrette. Mix together.

8. To serve, cut the lobster tails into six pieces. Arrange ten slices of potato around the outer edge of your largest dinner plate. Place a piece of tail meat on top of six of the potato slices. Lay the claw meat down on top of the remaining four slices. With a teaspoon, spoon a little mayonnaise between each potato slice. Place a little tomato dice on top of the mayonnaise and arrange a small handful of salad in the middle of the plate. Serve immediately.

Grilled Lobster with Garlic Butter

I buy between 70 and 100 lobsters a week from my man Carl for The New Angel and I have to say that they are definitely the sweetest ones that I have ever tasted. It's best to go for average-sized lobsters – the bigger ones can start to get a little tough, but they are still great minced for lots of lobster dishes, such as mousses, terrines or tortellini.

Serves 2

2 x 600-g live lobsters
250 g unsalted butter
3 garlic cloves
2 sprigs tarragon
1 bunch chervil, finely chopped
6 sprigs parsley, finely chopped
1 pinch cayenne pepper
juice of 1 lemon
salt and freshly milled black pepper
50 ml olive oil
50 g lettuce leaves
1 teaspoon Tarragon Vinaigrette (see
    page 219)
1 shallot, finely chopped

1. Put the butter into a mixing bowl and beat until soft and pale in colour. Peel the garlic and, on a chopping board, crush the cloves with the heel of a knife. Add a pinch of salt, then chop the garlic into a fine paste. Add to the butter.

2. Place a pan of water on the stove to boil. Pick the leaves from the tarragon stalks and blanch in boiling water for 30 seconds. Refresh under cold water, dry on kitchen paper, then chop. Add to the softened butter, along with the chervil, parsley, cayenne pepper and lemon juice. Check the seasoning and add salt and pepper if necessary. Refrigerate until needed.

3. Using a sharp knife, cut the lobsters in half, lengthways. Carefully remove the brain sac and entrail lines, which look like brown thread and run down through the tail of the lobster.

4. Turn the grill on full. Heat a large metal-handled frying pan on top of the stove. Crack the lobster claws using a heavy metal implement or rolling pin. Be careful during this process just to crack the shell and not to hit the claws so severely that you crush the flesh. Add the olive oil to the pan and, as soon as it starts to smoke, place the lobster in the pan, shell side down, and cook for 4 minutes. Season the flesh with salt and pepper and then place the pan under the grill. Grill for another 4 minutes, then remove and put to one side for 5 minutes to relax.

5. Remove the garlic butter from the refrigerator and cover the flesh of the lobsters with the butter. Grill for a further 2 minutes until the butter melts.

6. Toss the salad leaves with the vinaigrette and shallot in a bowl. Carefully place a handful of salad at the top of each plate. Place half a lobster either side of the salad and serve.

Shellfish Pasta

This dish can be served as an hors d'oeuvre or as a lunchtime or supper dish. Serve with a salad and, for added effect, spoon it into some old scallop shells. I like to grate Parmesan cheese over mine. I have chosen a mixture of mussels, clams and cockles for this dish, but you can use any shellfish, including scallops, lobster or crab. Most clams and cockles that come from the fishmongers are purified already. If you have gathered them yourselves, however, you will need to put them in buckets, covered in floured water overnight. The flour acts as a cleaning agent and gets rid of all the grit in the shells.

Serves 6 as a main course or 10 as a starter

1 kg mussels (shell weight)
600 g clams (shell weight)
400 g cockles (shell weight)
60 ml olive oil
60 g butter
1 onion, finely chopped
1 leek, finely chopped
1 stick celery, finely chopped
½ bulb fennel, finely chopped
3 garlic cloves, crushed and finely chopped
1 sprig fresh thyme
1 bay leaf
1 sprig fresh tarragon
freshly milled black pepper
1 glass dry white wine
1 pinch saffron
1 dessertspoon unsalted butter mixed with 1 dessertspoon plain flour
100 ml double cream
1 teaspoon chopped flat-leaf parsley
2 tomatoes, peeled, seeded and diced
1 pinch cayenne pepper
lemon juice
500 g pasta (see page 219), cut into spaghetti or tagliatelle

1. First, scrape the mussels, remove their beards and any barnacles attached to the surface of the shells, then wash in lots of cold running water. Tap any open shells on the work surface and discard the ones that refuse to close. Strain and put to one side.

2. Wash the clams and cockles in water and strain them into a colander. Keep the clams separate from the cockles.

3. Heat the olive oil in a large lidded saucepan on the stove and, as soon as it starts to smoke, add the butter. Immediately add the onion, leek, celery, fennel, garlic, thyme, bay leaf and tarragon. Stir to soften but not colour. Season with pepper, pour in the white wine and bring to the boil. When boiling, add the mussels and clams. Stir them into the vegetables and wine and cover with the lid. Cook for 2 minutes, then uncover, add the cockles, stir again, replace the lid and cook for a further 2–3 minutes. As soon as the shells begin to open, remove the pan from the heat, and strain the contents through a colander set over a bowl to catch the juices. Remove the fish from the shells, place in a bowl and set aside. Discard the shells.

4. Pour the juices through a fine sieve lined with a muslin cloth into a small pan. Bring to the boil and continue to boil until the liquid has been reduced by half. Add a large pinch of saffron. Cut the butter and flour mixture into small pieces and, piece by piece, whisk them in to thicken the sauce. Add the cream and return to the boil. Add the parsley and

tomato dice. Season with a pinch of cayenne pepper and a few drops of lemon juice. Remove the pan from the heat.

5. Meanwhile, cook the pasta for about 10 minutes, until it is al dente. Strain it through a colander and return it to the pan. Add the seafood and stir in the sauce. Turn out immediately into a serving dish.

Variation
You can also try a little diced, fresh red chilli in the mixture, or try replacing the saffron with curry paste.

Chapter
2. Fish

South Devon has a long-held fishing tradition dating back to medieval times, and though this has, sadly, largely declined, many towns, such as Brixham – which still has one of the best local fish markets – and Paignton, still run thriving local businesses, with brightly coloured hand-painted boats going out for their daily catch. And with fish, as with shellfish, the combination of salt and fresh water at the local river estuaries works its wonders, producing a fantastic range of fresh- and seawater fish, such as trout, perch, wild salmon and sea bass. At The New Angel, we have become particularly attached to the skate, turbot and mackerel, along with Torbay sole, a lighter variation of the highly prized Dover sole, with slightly sweeter flesh. These are all caught locally.

The fishing industry may have declined, but fish is still very much the order of the day here. One of the annual highlights of the Dartmouth calendar is the Plaice Festival, held in May

MOBY NICKS

Fishmongers

Chunky Monk £4.50/lb

Cornish Hake £4.77/lb

Dressed Crab £3.20 each

Today's Specials

Doing the daily fish buy here is a real joy. Even the smallest of fishmongers has the most wonderful varieties – brought straight from the local market in Brixham, often still glistening with seawater. I love experimenting with new techniques and recipes – see page 55 if you'd like to know how I use the smoked cod pictured above.

each year, in which friends and families go out plaice fishing over a weekend. The competitors bring in their catch on the Sunday, for a ceremonial weighing of the fish at 5 pm. The winner is the one who's caught the best fish in terms of length and weight – definitely a case where size matters! It can be a spectacular event, with more than 50 boats taking part. We entered for the first time this year and, to our great amazement and delight, Eliza caught a fish, her first ever – a 400-g plaice. She was over the moon.

Eliza is definitely the fish girl of the family. Otherwise, as with shellfish, fish-eating is a pleasure I'm mostly destined to enjoy on my own, though I have had some slight success with Charles, who likes cod and chips! Happily, however, my family's tastes don't seem to be reflected nationally, where fish-eating seems to be on the up – something I'm delighted about, as fish is my absolutely favourite food.

Many people are still a bit apprehensive about cooking fish – perhaps rightly so, because the difference between well and badly cooked fish can often come down to a matter of seconds. The best advice I can offer here is to start with an easy method, such as grilling or steaming, and to master that first. Just cook the fish until the flesh is firm, white and falls off the bone while still being moist. Couldn't be simpler.

Smoked Salmon Blinis

This is delicious as a light lunch, accompanied by a nice cold Chablis. You need a good smoked salmon and a pot of natural Greek yoghurt. The recipe makes twelve blinis and you should allow at least three for each person. Make sure you always serve them warm.

Serves 4 as a starter or light lunch

10 g yeast

75 g buckwheat flour

½ teaspoon salt

150 ml warm milk

1 egg, separated

2 egg whites

3 tablespoons clarified unsalted butter
   (see page 218–9)

150 g sliced smoked salmon

150 g natural Greek yoghurt

freshly milled black pepper

1. Put the yeast, flour and salt in a bowl. Warm the milk (but do not allow it to boil), then pour it into the flour, whisking continuously to form a smooth, thick batter. Cover the bowl with a damp tea towel and put somewhere warm to prove for about 1 hour. The airing cupboard is a good place.

2. Put the separated egg white in a bowl and whisk it to a peak. When the batter has proved, stir in the egg yolk and then, with a large spoon, gently fold in the egg white. Leave to relax for 30 minutes before using.

3. Heat a heavy frying pan on top of the stove. Brush with a little clarified butter, and add a tablespoon of batter. Cook gently for 1–2 minutes, then carefully turn over to cook the other side. It should be a golden colour. Keep warm.

4. Continue until all the batter has been used up, then serve the blinis immediately with the finely sliced smoked salmon, some natural Greek yoghurt and topped with freshly milled black pepper.

Grilled Wild Salmon with Red Butter Sauce

Try this as an alternative to a butter sauce. The red wine gives the sauce a beautiful rich flavour, which in turn brings out the flavour of the wild salmon. Take care not to overcook the salmon: it should be very lightly – almost under – cooked, never dry. New potatoes are a lovely accompaniment.

Serves 4

1-kg salmon steak or 4 x 250-g pieces
2 shallots, chopped
500 ml full-bodied red wine
salt and freshly milled black pepper
250 g butter, chilled, cut into pieces
groundnut oil
watercress, to garnish

1. Preheat the oven to 220°C/425°F/Gas 7.

2. Place the shallots, the wine and a pinch of salt and some pepper in a saucepan. Bring to the boil and reduce until only 3 tablespoons of liquid remains. Remove the pan from the heat and whisk in a little of the cold butter. Place the saucepan back on a low heat and, when the butter has melted, add a little more, piece by piece. Season with salt and pepper. Strain to remove the shallots and keep warm. The sauce should never be allowed to boil.

3. Turn the grill on full and lay the salmon steaks on a tray. Baste with groundnut oil and season with salt and pepper. Place the tray under the grill and cook gently for 5 minutes each side, then transfer the salmon to the oven for about 12 minutes to finish cooking, turning the fish over once during this time.

4. Place the salmon in the middle of the plate, pour a little of the red butter sauce around the outside and garnish with some watercress.

Carpaccio of Salmon with Crunchy Vegetables

There are a lot of different marinades for salmon, the most popular being Gravadlax. In Gravadlax the sugar acts like a poultice, drawing out a lot of the minerals and also, in my opinion, the flavour of the fish. This marinade doesn't. It both flavours the salmon and, at the same time, cures it. Try to use wild salmon.

Serves 8

600-g salmon fillet (a thick piece off
    the bone – nearest the head is best)
20 g coarse sea salt
20 g caster sugar
juice of 1 lemon
1 garlic clove, peeled and finely sliced
1 teaspoon fennel seeds
2 juniper berries, crushed
1 teaspoon crushed black peppercorns
3 tablespoons olive oil

Vegetables
1 large courgette, cut into 3-mm dice
1 potato, peeled, diced and washed
1 large carrot, peeled and diced
1 fennel bulb, peeled and diced
2 stalks celery, peeled and diced
40 g French beans
1 shallot, finely chopped
½ garlic clove, finely chopped
salt and freshly milled black pepper
60 ml Tarragon Vinaigrette (see
    page 219)
30 ml marinade
2 large tomatoes, skinned, cored,
    deseeded and cut into small dice

1. Put the salt and sugar into a large bowl. Strain the lemon juice into the salt and sugar and stir together with a whisk. Add the garlic, along with the fennel seeds, juniper berries and black peppercorns.Whisk in the olive oil. Place the salmon on a plastic tray, flesh side down, and pour over the marinade. Cover with cling film and leave overnight in the refrigerator. Remove the salmon from the marinade and lay it on a clean chopping board. Using the back of a knife, gently scrape off all the peppercorns, fennel seeds and garlic. Brush the salmon with a little more olive oil and put back in the fridge on a clean tray. Keep the marinade for later use.

2. Next prepare the vegetables. Place the courgettes in a bowl. Put the potato in a small saucepan, cover with water, bring to the boil, then remove from the heat and strain into a fine sieve. Leave to cool. In a large saucepan of boiling, salted water blanch the vegetables in order of cooking times: 1 minute for the carrot, then add the fennel; 30 seconds later add the celery, then add the beans after a further 30 seconds. Strain immediately through a fine mesh strainer, refresh in cold water, strain again and then turn out onto clean kitchen paper to dry. When dry, add to the bowl containing the courgettes, then add the potato, shallot and garlic. Season with a little salt and pepper and finally add 30 ml of the tarragon vinaigrette and a little of the salmon marinade. Stir. Season the tomatoes and sprinkle them with 15 ml of the vinaigrette.

3. To serve, lay out eight large plates and spoon the crunchy diced vegetables into the centre of each. With the back of the spoon, flatten them to form an even base for the salmon. Remove the salmon from the refrigerator, lay it on a board and, using a sharp filleting knife, slice it as thinly as you can. Lay the sliced salmon on top of the vegetables. Using a small brush, carefully brush the salmon with the remaining 15 ml of vinaigrette. Spoon a little of the diced tomato onto the centre of the salmon and serve.

Plaice with Anchovy and Herb Butter

Serve this with a bowl of baby new potatoes, accompanied by a glass of Chardonnay.

Serves 4

4 x 400-g plaice

3 tablespoons olive oil

juice of ½ lemon

salt and freshly milled black pepper

Anchovy and Herb Butter

2 bunches watercress

1 large bunch flat-leaf parsley

20 g fresh tarragon

1 bunch chervil

1 bunch chives

1 garlic clove, peeled

30 g capers

6 anchovy fillets

2 tablespoons olive oil

250 g unsalted butter, cut into cubes

juice of ½ lemon

1 pinch cayenne pepper

250 g unsalted butter

1. First prepare the fish. Lay the fish on a board and, using a sharp knife, cut off the heads. Be careful not to waste any flesh. With a pair of fish scissors, trim the fins from both sides. Lay the fish dark side up on the board and, again using a sharp knife, make a shallow cut along the width of the narrow part of the tail. With a small clean cloth catch hold of the dark skin and, using your forefinger and thumb, pull off the skin from tail to head and discard. Pour half the oil onto a baking sheet and lay the fish on it, white skin side down. Drizzle the remaining oil over the fish. Sprinkle with lemon juice and season with salt and pepper. Put to one side.

2. Next prepare the anchovy and herb butter. Half fill a saucepan with water and bring to the boil. Trim off the watercress stalks and put the leaves in a bowl to one side. Wash and pick the parsley (a large handful) and set aside in another bowl. Pick the leaves from five tarragon stalks and again set aside. When the water is boiling, add the parsley and cook for 1 minute. Then add the tarragon leaves and cook for a further minute. Finally add the watercress leaves. Submerge them under the boiling water, then immediately remove the pan from the heat. Strain over a sink and quickly refresh in cold or iced water. Strain again and, using your hands, squeeze out all the water from the herbs to form a green ball. Put the blanched herbs into a liquidiser, and add the chervil, chives, garlic and capers (squeeze the vinegar out of the capers). Then add the anchovy fillets and the olive oil and blitz to form a smooth paste. Scrape this into a bowl using a spatula and set aside. Beat the butter until it turns pale in colour. Add the herb paste and mix it thoroughly into the butter. Add a little lemon juice and a large pinch of cayenne pepper.

3. To cook the fish, turn the grill on full. When hot, place the fish under the grill and cook for 5 minutes. Remove the fish and cover with the herb and anchovy butter. Turn down the grill by half and cook for a further 5 minutes. Serve immediately.

Goujons of Plaice with Tartare Sauce

This is a quick, inexpensive dish and the kids love it too. You can use sole instead of plaice, if you prefer, or a cheaper white fish such as pollock, whiting or haddock. My kids prefer the fish dipped in breadcrumbs, though they can also be coated in batter.

Serves 4 as a starter or 2 as a main course

600 g plaice fillets, skinned

salt and freshly milled black pepper

2 litres corn or sunflower oil, for deep-frying

100 g plain flour

2 eggs

2 tablespoons milk

150 g fresh white breadcrumbs

4 tablespoons Tartare Sauce (see page 217)

1. Lay the fillets flat on a chopping board and cut them, one at a time, at an angle, into strips 7.5 cm long by 1 cm wide. Put the goujons into a bowl and season them with salt and pepper.

2. Heat the oil in a large pan or deep-fat fryer to a temperature of 170–180°C/325–350°F. If using a saucepan, make sure it is no more than a third full.

3. Sieve the flour onto a tray. Crack the eggs into a bowl and beat them together with the milk until smooth. Pour this into another tray. Sprinkle the breadcrumbs into yet another tray. First dip the goujons into the flour, rolling them over so that they are well covered. Put them into a sieve or colander and shake off any excess. Next dip them into the beaten egg, and again roll them around to cover. Piece by piece, lift them out and drop them into the breadcrumbs. Shake the tray to ensure that they are thoroughly coated. Pick up the goujons one at a time, pat them between your hands, and place them on another tray lined with greaseproof paper.

4. When the oil is at the right temperature, carefully add half the goujons and fry for 6–7 minutes until coloured a golden brown. Remove the goujons with a slotted spoon and keep them warm in the oven whilst you fry the other half. Serve immediately with the tartare sauce, brown bread and butter, and lemon wedges.

Pan-fried Mackerel with Gooseberries

My favourite spot for fishing for mackerel is on Slapton beach at the end furthest away from Torcross. I usually have the best luck on a high tide, and at dusk you can't miss. They are most prolific from early May through to the summer. I usually take the three little ones with me, which gives them a chance to play on the beach while I fish. This dish is good with a bowl of new potatoes and a small mixed salad.

Serves 4

400 g gooseberries

60 g unsalted butter

50 g caster sugar

25 g root ginger, peeled, and finely chopped or grated

zest of 1 orange

4 medium-sized mackerel

salt and freshly milled black pepper

2 tablespoons olive oil

1. Wash the gooseberries and drain them through a colander. Melt half the butter in a small lidded pan and add the sugar. Stir in the fruit, then add the ginger and orange zest. Cover with the lid and cook over a gentle heat for about 5 minutes. Remove the lid and turn up the heat to evaporate the liquid, stirring occasionally. This will take a further 10 minutes. Keep warm.

2. Cut open the stomachs of the mackerel from the vent to the gills. Remove the insides of the fish and discard. Cut out the gills and, with a pair of fish scissors, cut off the fins and discard. Wash the fish under cold running water and dry with kitchen paper. Turn the fish on its side and fillet it, cutting either side of the backbone. Discard the bone and, using a pair of tweezers, pin-bone the fillets. Turn the mackerel fillets over and make a few shallow cuts across the skin, to aid even cooking. Season the fillets with salt and pepper.

3. Place a large frying pan on the stove to heat. Pour in the olive oil and, as soon as it starts to smoke, lay the mackerel, flesh side down, into the oil. Fry for 3–4 minutes until coloured golden brown, then turn them over and cook for a further 2 minutes. Add the remaining butter. They are ready as soon as the butter has melted and started to foam.

4. Take the pan off the heat and, using a fish slice, remove the fillets and lay them on four serving plates. Serve immediately, with a spoonful of the gooseberry sauce on each plate.

Pickled Mackerel

This pickling vinegar can be used for other fish. If you are using herring, for example, you first should seal the fillets in hot nut-brown butter.

Serves 6

6 x 230-g mackerel
500 ml white distilled vinegar
20 g flat-leaf parsley
1 garlic clove
15 g black peppercorns
3 juniper berries
zest of 1 lemon (see method)
1 large onion
1 large carrot
1 stick celery
1 leek
½ bulb fennel
60 g caster sugar
20 g salt
1 sprig fresh thyme
1 bay leaf
1 teaspoon fennel seeds
1 star anise
60 ml olive oil

1. First prepare the mackerel. Cut off all the fins with fish scissors. Lay the fish on a board and, with the blade of a sharp knife angled towards the head, scrape off all the scales. Turn the fish over and repeat the process. Using the scissors, carefully cut open the stomach. Remove the entrails, cut out the gills and discard. Wash the fish under cold running water, then dry thoroughly on some kitchen roll.

2. Using a sharp filleting knife, remove the fillets by making an incision just behind the head of the fish, following the contours of the skull. Cut along the back of the mackerel, head to tail, and carefully slice down, angling the knife towards the backbone. Take off the first fillet, turn the fish over and repeat. Discard the bones.

3. Lay the fillets in a deep tray. The next stage is to remove the pin bones, which run down the middle of the fillet. You can use a pair of fish tweezers or pliers, but I find that with fresh mackerel it is difficult to pull the bones out without damaging the flesh. So, using the filleting knife, just cut straight down the middle of the fillet lengthways, on both sides of the bones, and discard. This method has the added advantage of removing the bloodline at the same time.

4. Next prepare the pickling vinegar. Pick the leaves off the parsley, wash and dry. Peel and chop the garlic, crush the peppercorns with the back of a small frying pan, and do the same for the juniper berries. Blanch the lemon zest for about 3 minutes in boiling water, strain it through a fine sieve and slice into fine strips. Set aside.

5. Slice the onion into rings as finely as possible. Peel the carrot and, with a canelle knife (single-grooved zester), cut out some grooves lengthways at regular intervals. Again, as finely as possible, cut it into rings. Peel the celery and slice across the grain into fine strips. Wash the leek, remove the outside leaves, cut off the green top, discard, and slice the same way. Top and tail the fennel, cut it into four, remove the core, separate the leaves and finely slice. Put all the vegetables into a large glass or stainless steel bowl, pour on the vinegar, add the sugar, salt, thyme, bay leaf, fennel seeds and star anise and stir, making sure that the sugar and salt is completely dissolved. Add the parsley leaves, crushed peppercorns and juniper berries. Add the lemon zest and whisk in the olive oil. Pour the pickling vinegar and all the vegetables over the mackerel, cover with cling film, and leave to marinate overnight.

6. To serve, remove the cling film. Transfer the mackerel to individual plates if you wish. Serve some of the vinegar and vegetable garnish with each portion.

Blackened Mackerel with Herb Mayonnaise

Mackerel, mackerel everywhere! Even if you are not a competent fisherman, you can't fail to catch one. When I go bass fishing and try and get my bait down to the bottom it usually doesn't make it and I end up bringing in a mackerel! It's not surprising, therefore, that they are pretty cheap to buy. Despite this, they are a great fish to eat, and easy to cook – simple is always best, I think, as far as fish is concerned. I like to serve this with baby new potatoes in their skins and spinach.

Serves 4

4 large mackerel, gutted and
    butterflied
3 garlic cloves, peeled and crushed
10 g black peppercorns, crushed
1 pinch salt
10 g Cajun spice
2 teaspoons paprika
3 tablespoons olive oil
1 sprig tarragon leaves
½ bunch chervil
2 sprigs parsley
170 g Mayonnaise (see page 218)
juice of ¼ lemon

1. First you need to butterfly the mackerel. Place the fish on a board and, working from the inside of the belly, run the knife either side of the backbone, cutting through the fine bones. Gently pull the backbone away, being careful not to take too much flesh away with it. Open out the fish, flesh side up, and remove any large bones on each side of the fillet.

2. In a bowl, mix the garlic with the crushed peppercorns, salt, Cajun spice and paprika.

3. Pour the olive oil into a large roasting tray and place the fish on it, skin side down. Spread the spices over each fish, pressing down lightly. Turn the grill on full.

4. Blanch the tarragon leaves for 2 minutes in boiling water, then refresh in cold water, strain and squeeze dry. Chop the tarragon, chervil and parsley and mix with the mayonnaise. Add a dash of lemon juice, if required.

5. Place the roasting tray under the grill and cook the mackerel for 5–8 minutes until cooked through. Place the fish on a large dinner plate. Serve the mayonnaise separately.

Grilled Red Mullet Fillets with Rosemary Cream Sauce

This dish can be served either as a starter or a main course; allow two fillets per person for a main course. I like to serve this with a mound of mashed potatoes piped through a piping bag with a large plain nozzle onto the centre of each plate. Place the fillets of red mullet on top of the potato and top each one with a tiny piece of liver. You can also place a small sprig of rosemary on top for added colour. Ratatouille also makes a delicious accompaniment to this dish if serving as a main course. Serve it separately in a bowl.

Serves 4

4 red mullet fillets from 2 x 350-g fish
1 tablespoon olive oil
salt and freshly milled black pepper
lemon juice

Rosemary Sauce
40 g unsalted butter
2 sprigs rosemary
1 garlic clove, peeled and chopped
125 ml Chicken Stock (see pages 213–14)
125 ml Fish Stock (see page 214)
125 ml double cream
salt
lemon juice

1. First prepare the red mullet. Cut off all the fins using fish scissors, then, using the back of a small knife, scrape off all the scales (tail to head) and discard. With the scissors, open up the stomach and discard all the entrails, but keep the livers and wash them under cold running water, then dry and set aside in a bowl. Cut out the gills, wash the fish and place on kitchen paper to dry.

2. Turn the mullet on its side and make an incision at the head. Following the contours of the head, slice along its side, the knife angled towards the backbone. Cut off the first fillet, turn the fish over, and remove the second fillet. With a pair of fish pliers or eyebrow tweezers remove the small bones running down the middle of the fillet. Place the fillets, skin side up, onto a flat baking sheet. Pour over a little of the olive oil, season with salt and black pepper, squeeze over a little lemon juice and put to one side.

3. Next prepare the sauce. Melt the butter in a pan and, as soon as it starts to froth and turn nut brown, add first the sprigs of rosemary and then the garlic. Pour in the chicken and fish stock, bring to the boil and reduce the liquid by half or until it becomes sticky and syrupy. Whisk in the cream and bring

the sauce back to the boil. Continue to boil the sauce until it is thick enough to coat the back of a spoon. Add a pinch of salt and a squeeze of lemon juice to taste. Strain the sauce into another small pan and discard the rosemary and garlic.

4. Place the red mullet fillets under a very hot grill and cook for 5 minutes. Meanwhile, if serving with mashed potato, take another small

pan and heat a little olive oil. Fry the livers for a few seconds just to seal them, then remove them from the pan. Place them on a board, cut into two and put on top of the fish. Spoon the rosemary sauce around the fish and serve immediately.

Haddock in Batter

This is delicious served with some Tartare Sauce (see page 217), home-made chips and a glass of dry white wine or a pint of lager. Fish is always best served straight from the fryer, but, as most people won't have a fryer big enough to contain eight pieces in one go, you may have to fry the fish in batches of four. Keep cooked pieces warm on a baking tray lined with greaseproof paper in an oven preheated to 160°C/325°F/Gas 3.

Serves 8

8 x 200-g haddock pieces, preferably
    from a big fish, bones removed,
    skin on
juice of ½ lemon
salt and freshly milled black pepper
450 g self raising flour, plus extra for
    dusting
2 eggs
500 ml lager
corn oil

1. Feel the top of the fish with your thumb for bones. Remove any you find using fish pliers or eyebrow tweezers. Lay the haddock on a tray, sprinkle each piece with some lemon juice and season with a little salt and pepper.

2. Sift the flour into a bowl. Make a well in the centre and crack into it the two eggs. Add a little lager and, using a whisk, beat the ingredients together to form a smooth paste. Gradually whisk in the remaining lager, a little at a time, until you achieve the consistency of a Yorkshire pudding batter. If the batter is too thin it will fall off the fish but if it is too thick there will be lumps of uncooked flour.

3. Heat the oil in a deep-fat fryer or large pan until it reaches a temperature of 180°C/350°F, making sure the pan is no more than a third full. Meanwhile, sprinkle a little flour on another tray. Put the haddock, flesh side down, onto the flour. Sprinkle a little more flour over the skins. Take each piece of fish and pat off the excess flour between your hands. Then, one piece at a time, dip the haddock into the batter, holding it between your forefinger and thumb, and carefully drop it into the hot oil. Fry for about 5 minutes or until golden brown. Serve immediately.

Smoked Haddock and Avocado Salad

This makes a refreshing, light lunch dish any time of the year. Buy a good, undyed smoked haddock.

Serves 4 or 4–6 as a starter

200 g undyed smoked haddock

200 ml milk

50 g cucumber

salt

30 g red pepper, peeled, seeded and cut into 5-mm dice

1 shallot, finely chopped

50 g new potatoes

5 g flat-leaf parsley, chopped

25 g Mayonnaise (see page 218)

Topping

50 g soured cream, thick set

10 g freshly grated horseradish

salt

cayenne pepper

lemon juice

Garnish

1 tomato, peeled, seeded and diced

50 ml Tarragon Vinaigrette (see page 219)

cayenne pepper

1 sprig fresh chervil

2 ripe avocados, peeled and cut into 3-mm slices

1. Place the haddock in a pan and cover with the milk. Poach lightly on the stove for about 10 minutes. Remove the fish from the milk, peel off the skin whilst it is still warm, and carefully flake the flesh into a bowl.

2. Peel the cucumber and cut it into two, lengthways, then deseed and marinate it in salt for 20 minutes. Wash under cold running water, dry thoroughly with kitchen paper and dice into 5-mm cubes. Add it to the haddock, along with the diced pepper and shallot.

3. In a small saucepan, boil the potatoes for 20 minutes or until tender. Strain, allow to cool slightly, then, whilst they are still hot, peel and dice into 5-mm cubes. Stir into the haddock mixture, along with the parsley. Bind everything together with the mayonnaise.

4. Put the soured cream in a small bowl and stir in the horseradish. Season with a little salt, cayenne pepper and lemon juice. Set aside in the refrigerator.

5. Place four 5.5-cm ring moulds on four large plates. Spoon the haddock mixture into the moulds and press it down; it should fill the moulds to within about 5 mm of the top. Spoon a dessertspoon of soured, horseradish cream over the tops of the ring moulds and, with a small palette knife, smooth the cream over the haddock to make them level. Carefully remove the ring moulds and top each with a little tomato dice mixed with half of the tarragon vinaigrette. Sprinkle a pinch of cayenne on top and finish it with a small leaf of chervil. Pour the remaining vinaigrette into another

bowl, add the avocados, and carefully turn them over so that they are completely covered in the dressing. Place the avocado slices, overlapping each other, around the bottom of the haddock. Serve immediately.

Applewood-smoked Cod with Seed Mustard Butter

This method of smoking fish goes back hundreds of years. You can buy applewood shavings from most good garden centres. When cooking this dish, use a very old pan, keep the windows open and turn off the smoke alarm!

Serves 4

300 g French beans or sugar snap
    peas, topped and tailed
1 dessertspoon seed mustard
150 ml Butter Sauce, freshly prepared
    (see page 216)
4 x 200-g cod portions (use the
    thickest pieces from just behind the
    head)
250 g applewood shavings or chips
1 tablespoon olive oil
30 g unsalted butter
salt and freshly milled black pepper

Variation

A poached egg on top of the cod is a delicious addition. For instructions on how to poach an egg, see page 145.

1. First make the garnish. Half fill a large saucepan with water. Add a good pinch of salt and cover. When the water is boiling, add the beans, replace the lid for a few moments and, as soon as the water is boiling again, uncover. Cook the beans for about 4 minutes or until tender with just a bite. Remove the pan from the heat and strain the beans. Refresh them in cold, or iced, water and, when cold, strain again and set aside. Stir the mustard into the butter sauce. Set aside but keep warm.

2. Put your old pan on the stove over a fierce flame and cover. Meanwhile, place the pieces of cod on a wire rack. Once the pan is very hot, pour in the wood shavings. Lay the rack with the cod over the shavings and replace the lid. As the wood burns, the smoke will cure the fish. Smoke the cod for 10 minutes. Lift the lid, remove the rack with the cod on it and put to one side. The fish will look partly cooked and smell delicious. Carefully take the pan outside to cool. There will be a lot of smoke.

3. Put a large frying pan on the stove. Add the olive oil and heat it until it starts to smoke. Using a fish slice, very carefully lay the fish topside down in the pan. Cook to colour the fish a crisp golden brown. This should take about 3 minutes. Place another small pan on the stove and melt the butter. Add the beans and some seasoning, and toss them in the butter to reheat. Turn the cod over and cook the other side. Warm the mustard sauce to just below boiling point, but do not boil it. Spoon the beans onto the centre of each plate, place the cod on top and spoon over a generous amount of mustard sauce.

Fillets of Lemon Sole with Cockles and Parsley

Cockles, because of the nature of their habitat, are usually full of grit. Clean them as described on page 28.

Serves 6

3 x 650-g large lemon sole or 12 large
   fillets, skinned

1.75 kg cockles (shell weight), soaked
   overnight

140 ml olive oil

60 g unsalted butter

1 large onion

2 garlic cloves, peeled and chopped

15 g black peppercorns, crushed

1 glass dry white wine

1 bay leaf

1 large sprig fresh thyme

60 g parsley stalks

100 ml Fish Stock (see page 214)

80 ml double cream

60 g flat-leaf parsley, finely chopped

2 large ripe plum tomatoes, blanched,
   skinned and diced

lemon juice

60 g plain flour

salt and freshly milled black pepper

1. Put a large, lidded saucepan on the stove over a fierce heat. Pour in 80 ml of olive oil and, as soon as it starts to smoke, add the butter to melt but not colour. Add the onion, garlic and peppercorns. Pour in the wine, and add the bay leaf, thyme and parsley. Add the cockles, cover, and cook for 5 minutes. Stir the cockles from bottom to top once or twice during this time. Turn out the cockles into a colander placed over a bowl to trap the cooking juices. Strain the cooking juices through muslin to trap any sand that may have come out during cooking. Remove the cockles from the shells, and pull off and discard the grit sac. Set aside.

2. Pour the strained cooking juices into a small pan and bring to the boil to reduce. As soon as the liquid becomes syrupy, add the fish stock, return to the boil, and add the cream. Continue to boil the sauce until it is thick enough to coat the back of a spoon, then reduce the heat and keep warm. Add the finely chopped parsley and tomatoes, plus a little lemon juice to bring out the flavours. Put the prepared cockles into the sauce and stir.

3. Meanwhile, put two large frying pans on the stove to heat. Sieve the flour onto a large tray and season with salt and black pepper. Dust the lemon sole fillets in the flour and shake off any excess. Pour the remaining olive oil into the pans and, as soon as they start to smoke, carefully lay the fillets in the pans and cook for 2–3 minutes on each side until coloured a light golden brown. When cooked, place two fillets on each plate and spoon the cockles and sauce over them. Serve immediately.

Pan-fried Torbay Sole with Capers and Parsley

The only difference I can detect between a Torbay sole and a Dover sole is the colour. Torbay sole, as they are called in these parts, are fished off the sandbanks not far from Torbay. They are much lighter in colour – an almost sandy brown as opposed to the darker-skinned Dover sole. The fishermen here say they are sweeter because they come from clean water! I like to serve this dish with either new or mashed potatoes. A salad also makes a lovely accompaniment.

Serves 4

4 x 500-g Torbay sole
2 tablespoons plain flour
salt and freshly milled black pepper
100 ml olive oil
125 g unsalted butter
100 ml Chicken Stock
   (see pages 213–14)
juice of 1 lemon
2 dessertspoons capers
1 dessertspoon flat-leaf parsley,
   chopped

1. Remove the fins of the sole using some sharp fish scissors. Cut off the heads and discard. Turn the sole over and make a small shallow incision about ½ cm up from the tail, just nicking the darker coloured skin. Take a piece of kitchen paper between your thumb and forefinger. Grab the skin and pull it towards the head as fast as possible removing the skin in one. Discard.

2. Sprinkle the flour onto a tray. Season it with salt and pepper. Lay the prepared soles in the flour, then shake off the excess by patting them between your hands and place on a clean tray.

3. Preheat the oven to 200°C/400°F/Gas 6.

4. Place two large frying pans onto the stove to heat. Add 50 ml of oil to each pan and, as soon as it starts to smoke, lay the sole, skinned side down, into the oil. Fry for about 3 minutes on each side. They should be golden brown in colour. Remove with a fish slice and lay on a baking sheet, skinned side up. Put in the oven to keep warm.

5. Divide the butter and add it to the pans. As it starts to melt, bubble and turn a nut-brown colour, pour in the chicken stock. Boil and reduce the sauce until it becomes syrupy. Squeeze in the lemon juice and add the capers and parsley.

6. Remove the soles from the oven and place them onto four large dinner plates. Spoon the sauce over the sole and serve immediately.

Fillet of Brill with Oysters

The brill that the day-boat fishermen bring me for the restaurant are the best I have ever seen. There is no fish stock in this dish, which I usually prepare for a lunchtime menu – the only juice is what comes out of the fish and oysters into the wine during cooking. I like to serve it with a glass of whatever I have cooked the fish in; Riesling or Gewürztraminer work best, but, if you are feeling rich, use Champagne! New potatoes or a plain pasta work well as an accompaniment.

Serves 4

4 x 175-g brill, filleted and skinned
110 g unsalted butter
1 shallot, finely chopped
salt and freshly milled black pepper
125 ml dry white wine
juice of ¼ lemon
16 oysters, in their shells
1 large carrot, peeled and cut into
    8-cm long matchstick strips
1 leek, peeled and cut into 8-cm long
    matchstick strips
1 celery stick, peeled and cut into
    8-cm long matchstick strips

Variation
This recipe can also be used for turbot, monkfish, seabass and lobster.

1. Preheat the oven to 190°C/375°F/Gas 5.

2. Use 25 g of the butter to grease an ovenproof ceramic dish. Sprinkle the shallot over the base of the dish, then season the fish with salt and pepper and lay them on top of the shallot. Pour over the wine and lemon juice, cover the dish with a sheet of greaseproof paper and place in the oven to poach for about 10 minutes.

 3. Remove the dish from the oven and carefully take out the fillets. Set aside and keep warm. Strain the cooking juices through a fine sieve into a small bowl.

4. Open the oysters, remove their beards and place them in a bowl. Strain the oyster juice through a fine sieve lined with a muslin cloth to trap any bits of shell. Pour the juice over the oysters and put to one side until needed.

5. Put the carrot, leek and celery sticks into a frying pan with another 25g of the butter and cook them gently over a moderate heat, but don't allow them to colour. When tender, pour in the cooking juices and bring to the boil. Add the oysters and cook for just 15 seconds. Remove the pan from the heat and, with a slotted spoon, quickly remove the vegetables and oysters and arrange them over the brill.

6. Boil the stock until its volume has been reduced by half. Continue boiling and whisk in the remaining butter, cut into dice. Check the seasoning, then pour the sauce over the fish and oysters. Serve immediately.

Brill with Seed Mustard and Green Peppercorn Sauce

I like to eat this dish with some shredded runner beans and new potatoes. Asparagus spears or young spinach leaves also work well, as do steamed buttered baby leeks and carrots.

Serves 4

4 x 150-g brill fillets, skinned
salt and freshly milled black pepper
lemon juice
200 ml Fish Stock (see page 214)
50 ml double cream
30 g unsalted butter, cut into small cubes
1 teaspoon green peppercorns
1 teaspoon seed mustard
1 small bunch chives, finely chopped

1. Preheat the oven to 180°C/350°F/Gas 4.

2. Lay the brill fillets on a plate. Season and sprinkle with a little lemon juice.

3. Pour the fish stock into a frying pan that can subsequently go in the oven, and bring it to the boil. Place the brill in the stock, cover with a sheet of greaseproof paper, and put in the oven for about 7 minutes to bake.

4. Using a fish slice, remove the brill from the pan and place in a warm serving dish. Strain the stock through a fine sieve into another small frying pan and boil to reduce it by half. Pour in the cream and whisk. Add the butter, piece by piece, whisking it into the sauce. Keep it boiling all the time.

5. Add the green peppercorns. Reduce the heat to a gentle simmer – the sauce must not boil at this stage or it will split and curdle – and stir in the seed mustard. Sprinkle the chives into the sauce, season with a little salt and a squeeze of lemon juice, then pour over the fish and serve.

Whole Grilled Sea Bass in Salt Pastry

I have included this recipe for two reasons. Firstly, during the season (May to the end of September) bass are everywhere in Dartmouth and are very popular and sell extremely well. Secondly, it is one of my friend's, Pat Llewelyn's, favourite dishes. I know that if I include it in the book her husband, Ben, will attempt to make it. Serve it with a Butter Sauce (see page 216), flavoured with chopped chives, accompanied by fresh pasta or new potatoes, and green beans or a salad.

Serves 6

3 x 750–800-g sea bass

50 g dill or fennel top

1 egg, beaten together with 30 ml milk, for egg wash

30 g unsalted butter, melted

Salt Crust Pastry

1 kg plain flour

600 g table salt

20 g dried fennel seeds

300 ml egg whites (about 10 eggs)

300 ml water

1. First make the salt crust pastry. Sieve the flour into the bowl of a food mixer and attach the dough hook. Add the salt and fennel seeds and mix together with the motor set at its lowest speed. Add the egg whites and continue mixing for 2–3 minutes. Gradually add the water and mix until you have a smooth pastry that comes away cleanly from the sides of the bowl. Stop the machine, turn out the pastry and wrap it up tightly in cling film. Put to one side to rest for at least 30 minutes.

2. Preheat the oven to 220°C/425°F/Gas 7.

3. Clean, gut and scale the bass. With a pair of fish scissors, cut off the fins and trim the tail fins. Dry the remaining fish on some kitchen paper.

4. Lightly dust a work surface with a little flour. Cut the salt crust into six equal pieces and, in turn, cut these in half. Roll out each piece into a rectangle 32 x 20 cm, with a thickness of about 5 mm. Lay the bass lengthways in the middle of three of the rectangles. Place some dill or fennel tops into the stomach of the fish. Dip a small pastry brush into cold water and brush around the edges of the pastry. Place a second piece of pastry over the fish and, using the sides of your hands, gently mould and shape the pastry so that the contours of the fish are visible. Press the edges down firmly to seal the pastry tightly; there must not be any holes. The fish cooks in its own steam and if there are any holes in the pastry you will not achieve the correct result.

Cut away the overlapping excess pastry around the fish. When doing this remodel the fins and cut out a tail. Leave a border of about 1 cm of pastry between the fins to allow for shrinkage during cooking. With the back of a knife score the fins to give a more authentic appearance. Take some of the excess pastry, roll it out and cut another fin. With the pastry brush, brush a little more water just behind the gill and press this onto the pastry. Mould an eye and again, with a little water, stick it in place. Gently drag the point of your knife along the middle of the fish, stopping just at the back of the head. To mould some scales, start at the tail of the fish and, with the point of your knife, pit the pastry all the way up to the head. Repeat this process several times for maximum effect but be very careful not to puncture the pastry. Brush the pastry with egg wash and place on a baking tray.

5. Cook in the preheated oven for 17 minutes, then remove the fish from the oven and brush the salt crust with the melted butter. Transfer the fish to a board and present them to your table.

6. To remove the fish from the pastry, cut, using a sharp knife, around the outer edge of the crust (the skin will automatically come away as well). With a sharp knife and fork, remove the top fillet to a serving plate. Remove and discard the exposed backbone, gently lift out the remaining fillet and place on another plate. Serve immediately.

Whitebait

Whitebait is the 'fry' of the common herring. The season runs from late March to August. I rarely see fresh ones on the market but frozen fish work just as well. It is very important to keep the oil temperature constant. If you attempt to fry the fish all in one batch the temperature of the oil will fall too much and the result will be a big ball of greasy fish! Serve with brown bread and butter and wedges of lemon.

Serves 6

750 g–1 kg whitebait
oil or lard for frying
500 ml milk
60 g plain flour
salt and freshly milled black pepper
1 large pinch cayenne pepper

1. Heat the oil or lard in a deep-fat fryer or large pan until it reaches a temperature of 190–200°C/375–400°F, making sure that the fryer or pan is no more than one third full.

2. Pour the milk into a bowl and add a third of the whitebait. It's always best to cook these fish in small numbers; they are very fragile and must be treated gently.

3. Lay a sheet of greaseproof paper over a large tray and sieve the flour onto it. Season the flour with some salt, some freshly milled black pepper and some cayenne pepper.

4. Lift the whitebait from the milk using a slotted spoon and, one by one, place in the flour. Make sure that they do not touch each other. Place them in a large sieve over the tray and gently shake off any excess flour, making sure that they are completely covered.

5. Fry the coated whitebait in the very hot oil or fat for about 1 minute or until crisp and coloured. Shake off any excess oil and place on some kitchen paper to drain. Repeat the process for the remaining whitebait. Serve hot.

Fillet of Turbot with Herb Dressing

This dish works well with most flat fish and, if you can get it, wild salmon. Serve on a bed of new season fine asparagus or samphire. It works well as a main course but a smaller version can be served as a starter too. If you don't like sherry vinegar try balsamic.

Serves 4

4 x 150-g pieces of turbot, filleted and
    skinned
50 ml Fish Stock (see page 214)
100 ml olive oil, plus an extra 2
    tablespoons
2 tablespoons sherry vinegar
2 tomatoes, blanched, skinned cored
    and cut into 1-cm dice
1 teaspoon chopped chervil
1 bunch chives, chopped
salt and freshly milled black pepper
24 fine spears asparagus
lemon juice
20 g unsalted butter

1. First prepare the dressing. Put the fish stock in a bowl and whisk in the 100 ml of olive oil and the vinegar. Add the tomatoes. Stir in the chervil and chives, season with salt and pepper, and set aside.

2. Put a pan half filled with water on the stove to boil. If the asparagus spears are very fine it will not be necessary to peel them; young asparagus is not tough. Just cut off the bottoms about 2 cm up. Salt the boiling water and add the asparagus. Return to the boil, cook for 2 minutes, strain through a sieve or colander, then refresh the asparagus in cold water in a bowl. When cold, strain off the water and put to one side.

3. Season the fish with salt and pepper, and sprinkle with a little lemon juice. Place a large frying pan on the stove and add the 2 tablespoons of olive oil. As it starts to smoke, place the turbot fillets in the pan, topside down. Cook for about 3 minutes on each side until just coloured. (The exact cooking time will depend on the thickness of the fillets.) Add the butter and, as soon as it starts to foam, remove the fish from the pan, otherwise it will burn.

4. Pour the dressing into another pan and gently warm it on the stove. Do not allow it to boil.

5. Lay out four plates and place the asparagus, six spears per plate, in a criss-cross pattern in the centre of each. Place the hot turbot on top of the asparagus and spoon the dressing over the fish. Serve immediately.

Warm Salad of Skate

I think skate – which is fantastic both hot and cold – is best from October to April. It's one of the very few fish that is better cooked two or three days after it is caught.

Serves 4

4 x 250-g skate wings
300 g new potatoes
salt and freshly milled black pepper
120 g fresh broad beans, shelled
120 g fresh peas, shelled
60 g mint
100 ml Tarragon Vinaigrette
   (see page 219)
100 g mixed lettuce leaves
1 teaspoon finely chopped shallots or
   1 small onion, finely chopped
100 ml olive oil
lemon juice

1. Wash the skate wings under cold water, then dry thoroughly using kitchen paper. With a pair of fish scissors, trim about 1 cm around the edge of the wing and discard. Put the wings on a plate.

2. Wash and scrape the new potatoes. Half fill a small saucepan with water and bring to the boil. Season with salt. Cook the potatoes – they should take about 15 minutes. Put a small knife into one to check – the potato should just fall off the knife.

3. Preheat the oven to 230°C/450°F/Gas 8.

4. Blanch the broad beans in boiling salted water for about 3 minutes or until the water comes back to the boil. Strain through a sieve and then refresh in cold water. Strain again and remove the tough outer skins. Put to one side in a bowl. Cook the peas in boiling salted water until tender; this should take about 5 minutes. Refresh them in cold water and, when cold, strain and put in another bowl.

5. Pick the mint leaves from the stalks and chop very finely with a sharp knife. Stir it into the tarragon dressing and set aside. Strain the cooked potatoes and, whilst they are still warm, slice them into a bowl and pour over half the mint dressing. Place the lettuce leaves in a bowl, pour over half of the remaining dressing and mix thoroughly. You will need about 1 tablespoon. Sprinkle the shallots or onion over the lettuce.

6. Heat a large pan, and place a baking sheet in the oven to get hot. Add the olive oil to the frying pan and heat until it begins to smoke. Season the dry skate wings with salt and lots of black pepper. Fry the fish for 3 minutes per side, dark side down first. Remove the hot baking sheet from the oven and, using a fish slice, transfer the skate to the baking sheet. Pour the oil from the pan over the fish and cook it in the oven for about 10 minutes until it's golden brown and tender to the touch.

7. Lay out four large plates and spoon the minted potatoes onto the centre of each. Mix the broad beans and peas together, stir in the remaining mint dressing, then spoon around the potatoes. Remove the skate from the oven and transfer to a board. Carefully peel off the dark skin and discard. Lift the flesh off the bone by putting the knife between the bone and the flesh. Turn over and repeat the process. Sprinkle with a little lemon juice. Carefully lay the skate on top of the potatoes and top each one with a little lettuce. Serve immediately.

Chapter

3. Birds

"Roast chicken is a great family favourite. The minute I start carving, everyone starts clamouring for their favourite cuts." john

To my family, 'birds' invariably means only one thing: chicken. Roast chicken stuffed with sage and onion and served with all the trimmings is one of our favourite family Sunday lunches and, because there are eight of us, it means buying two birds every time. Kim and I like to leave them whole when they come sizzling out of the oven, and to carve them at the table. I love this informal, family-style way of eating, and it's something I really want to recreate at the restaurant – without the dramas that inevitably take place at home, of course.

The dramas begin when I start carving as everyone has a favourite part. I'm fairly relaxed about what I have, which helps, but the rest have very definite views: Charles and Kim always want a leg; Olivia, Eve and Martha usually end up fighting over the breasts. Then, just when Kim and I think it's all over, it starts again, as Charles, Eliza and Amelia enter

I've been delighted to find many Devon poultry farmers who have joined the ever-growing national movement towards rearing organic free-range birds, and many of the farms I've visited have had chickens literally everywhere – even perching on the farm equipment. Our all-time favourites at The New Angel are corn-fed chickens. Their buttery flavour is superb.

into a life-or-death struggle for the wishbones. And with only two chickens involved, there's always a loser.

In celebration of these riotous occasions, I've included my recipe for Roast Chicken with Sage and Onion Stuffing here. The chickens we use at The New Angel come from an organic farm in the nearby village of Chillington. Free-range and fed entirely on corn, we love them for their tender meat and sweet buttery flavour. We also serve duck – a great favourite with Kim and me, because it always brings back memories of the time when we lived in the Aude in southwestern France, where it's pretty much a staple.

Game birds also feature on our menus. The Duke of Somerset has a huge estate just outside Totnes that supplies us with mallard duck, pheasant and partridge, all of which are reared on grass and shot when in season. My own particular favourites are woodcock, pheasant and partridge, which I adore roasted as an alternative to chicken. This is strictly restricted to restaurant fare, however, as game is a dirty word as far as the children are concerned. I have been known, on occasion, to go out shooting game birds, for the table rather than for pleasure, but the children hate it. When Eliza sees my recently shot birds hanging up in the kitchen she won't speak to me for a week!

Breast of Chicken with a Tarragon Cream Sauce

Choose a good quality chicken – something free-range or organic. A corn-fed chicken is best; although expensive, it is well worth it. This dish is great with Sauté Potatoes (see page 136) or even rice. French beans or spinach make a lovely contrast to the richness of the sauce.

Serves 6

3 tarragon branches
6 x 175-g chicken breasts, skinned
salt and freshly milled black pepper
1 tablespoon olive oil
1 garlic clove, peeled and sliced
50 ml white wine
100 ml Chicken Stock
  (see pages 213–14)
100 ml double cream
35 g unsalted butter, cut into pieces
lemon juice, to taste

1. Preheat the oven to 200°C/400°F/Gas 6.

2. Put a small pan of water on the stove to boil. Put the tarragon leaves into the boiling water for 2 minutes. Strain into a sieve over a sink and refresh with cold water. Strain again and squeeze dry. Chop finely and put to one side.

3. Season the chicken breasts with a little salt and pepper. Heat a shallow ceramic ovenproof dish on the stove. Add the olive oil and place the chicken breasts skin side down into the oil to seal. Fry for 2 minutes and then turn over. Cover with butter papers or a sheet of foil and put in the oven for about 20 minutes. When cooked, remove from the oven and place in a shallow serving dish. Keep warm.

4. Put the cooking dish on the stove, add the garlic and pour in the white wine. Boil and reduce the wine until it becomes syrupy. Add the chicken stock and boil to reduce it by half, which will take about 10 minutes. Then whisk in the cream. Bring the sauce back to the boil, then strain it through a fine sieve into a small saucepan. Bring it back to the boil and stir in the tarragon. Stir in the butter, piece by piece, until it has melted into the sauce and add a little lemon juice, to taste. Pour the sauce over the chicken and serve.

Roast Chicken with Sage and Onion Stuffing

Use a free-range chicken for this dish, and get one with the neck and livers inside.

Serves 4

1 x 1.75-kg chicken

1 chicken neck

30 g chicken liver

salt and freshly milled black pepper

30 g unsalted butter, softened

4 rashers streaky bacon

75 ml groundnut oil

1 onion, roughly chopped

1 carrot, roughly chopped

1 stick celery, cut into three

1 leek, white part only, chopped

1 sprig sage

1 bay leaf

1 glass dry white wine

250 ml Chicken Stock
   (see pages 213–14)

1 bunch watercress, to garnish

Stuffing

50 g pork fat

2 onions, finely chopped

2 sprigs sage

115 g coarse white breadcrumbs

1 egg

salt and freshly milled black pepper

30 g unsalted butter, softened

Variation

As an alternative, you can add sausage meat to this stuffing. Add half of the total weight of sausage meat.

1. Preheat the oven to 190°C/375°F/Gas 5.

2. Remove the livers from the chicken and reserve. (You will need about 30 g.) Take out the neck, chop it into small pieces and set aside. Season the chicken with salt and pepper, brush with the softened butter and place the rashers of bacon on top.

3. Place a thick-bottomed roasting tray on the stove to heat. Add the groundnut oil and, as it starts to smoke, add the vegetables. Stir with a wooden spoon and add the chopped neck bone. Fry for about 5 minutes to slightly colour the vegetables. Add the sprig of sage and the bay leaf. Place the chicken on top of the vegetables and roast for about 1 hour 15 minutes.

4. Meanwhile make the stuffing. Melt the pork fat in a frying pan over a moderate heat. Add the onions and cook slowly until they are tender but with no colour. Remove the pan from the heat. Pick the leaves off the sage and chop as finely as possible. You need a good teaspoon full. Add the sage and breadcrumbs to the onions and stir together. Crack the egg into a small bowl and beat it with a fork until smooth. Stir the egg into the stuffing mixture to bind it. Season with a little salt and lots of pepper. Rub the inside of a small ovenproof dish with half the softened butter and spoon in the stuffing. Dot butter on top and cook in the oven for about 25 minutes.

5. When the chicken is cooked, put the roasting pan on top of the stove. Lift the chicken, tilting it to let the juices run out into the pan, then set aside to rest. Pour the wine into the pan with the vegetables and bring to the boil. Boil the wine and juices until they become syrupy. Add the chicken stock and bring back to the boil. Strain the sauce through a fine sieve over a small saucepan and discard the contents of the sieve. Bring the sauce back to the boil and, using a ladle, remove all the surfacing fats and scum. Reduce the heat to a moderate simmer. Chop the reserved chicken liver to a purée and add to the gravy. Stir it with a whisk and reduce the heat to a gentle simmer.

Cook for about 10 minutes, then strain the sauce first through a fine sieve and then through a muslin cloth. Transfer to a gravy boat. To serve, put the chicken on a serving board and dress it with a large bunch of watercress. Serve the stuffing and gravy separately.

Chicken in Red Wine

This makes a delicious dish all year round – I've put it on the lunch menu at The New Angel and it is very popular. Traditionally, the sauce was thickened with the extracted blood of the chicken. It was stirred into the sauce at a temperature below boiling point so that it didn't curdle. Nowadays, however, this method has been largely dispensed with. Mashed potatoes do a good job of mopping up the sauce. The only other accompaniment needed is a green vegetable.

Serves 8

2 x 1.5-kg chickens (marinated
   overnight)
1 bottle red wine
1 glass ruby port
1 onion, chopped
5 garlic cloves, 4 peeled and chopped,
   1 left whole
1 bay leaf
2 sprigs thyme
250 g bacon, cut into lardons 2 cm
   long x 0.5 cm wide
24 small shallots, peeled but left whole
750 ml Chicken Stock
   (see pages 213–14)
80 g unsalted butter
salt and freshly milled black pepper
1 pinch caster sugar
2 tablespoons groundnut oil
60 g plain flour
1 tablespoon tomato purée
250 g button mushrooms
1 French stick, cut into 24 slices
1 tablespoon chopped flat-leaf parsley

1. First joint the chicken into eight pieces. Cut off the legs, then cut each leg into two, cut down either side of the backbone and take the short breasts off. Then turn the chicken over and cut through the cartilage down the centre of the breastbone.

2. Pour the wine and the port into a large bowl. Add the onion and the chopped garlic, together with the bay leaf and thyme. Put in the chicken and cover the bowl with cling film. Marinate overnight in the refrigerator.

3. Bring a small saucepan of water to the boil. Add the bacon and blanch in the boiling water for about 2 minutes. Strain through a fine sieve and dry thoroughly with kitchen paper. Brown the bacon strips in a pan with a little of the oil, then set aside.

4. Place the shallots in a small saucepan with 3 tablespoons of the chicken stock, 40 g of the butter, some salt, pepper and a pinch of sugar. Cook on the stove until all the chicken stock has evaporated. The shallots should be brown and glazed. Place them in a bowl and reserve.

5. Preheat the oven to 190°C/375°F/Gas 5.

6. Drain the chicken through a colander over a large bowl. Reserve the marinade. Dry the chicken pieces on some kitchen paper. Season with salt and pepper. Place a large frying pan on the stove to heat. Add the groundnut oil and, as soon as it starts to smoke, add the chicken pieces and fry until a golden brown colour. Lift the chicken out of the pan with a slotted spoon and place in a casserole dish. Add the remaining butter to the frying pan. When it has melted, add the flour and stir together to form a paste. Stir in the reserved marinade and bring it to the boil, then continue to boil to reduce the liquid by half. Stir in the tomato purée. Pour the liquor over the chicken and stir in the chicken stock. Put the casserole on the stove and bring the liquid back up to the boil. With a ladle, skim off all the surfacing scum and foam and discard. Put a lid on the casserole and place it in the oven for about 45 minutes; 10 minutes from the end of cooking, give the chicken a stir and add the mushrooms, bacon lardons and glazed shallots. Replace the lid and return to the oven.

7. Place the slices of bread on a roasting tray. Sprinkle with olive oil and place in the oven to toast a golden brown. Remove from the oven. Cut the remaining clove of garlic in two and, using the heel of a small knife, score the cut sides. Rub each crouton with the garlic pieces and set aside.

8. Lay out eight warm dinner plates. Remove the chicken from the oven and, with a ladle, put two pieces of chicken and some sauce onto each plate. Dip the edges of the croutons firstly into the sauce and then into the chopped parsley and arrange them on top of the chicken.

Kids' Chicken Curry

The kids love a curry, especially on a cold winter's night. It is also great as an alternative to a Sunday roast in the summer. You can garnish the curry with a Malaysian-style sambal: roasted peanuts in their skins, sliced banana, boiled egg quarters, red onion rings, mango chutney and sliced fresh tomatoes. Serve with plain boiled basmati rice or an unpolished Thai variety and Naan Bread (see page 206). I like to make the curry the day before serving. As with a lot of casserole-type dishes, it always tastes better reheated. If left for a day or two the aromas have more time to flavour the meat and sauce.

Serves 8

2 x 1.5-kg chickens, each cut into eight pieces

4 tablespoons vegetable oil

3 onions, chopped

1 apple (Bramley or Granny Smith), peeled and finely diced

3 garlic cloves, peeled and chopped

20 g raw stem ginger, peeled and finely chopped

2 red peppers, seeded and diced

2 green peppers, seeded and diced

1 tablespoon tomato purée

1 teaspoon cumin powder

15 g mild (Korma) curry powder or paste

20 g hot (Madras) curry powder or paste

1 cinnamon stick

400 ml coconut milk

1 tablespoon mango chutney

500 ml Chicken Stock (see pages 213–14)

1.4 kg small King Edward potatoes, peeled

1. Preheat the oven to 220°C/425°F/Gas 7.

2. Heat a large frying pan. Add half the vegetable oil and fry half of the chicken to a golden brown colour; this will take about 10 minutes. With a slotted spoon, transfer the pieces to a colander placed over a bowl to drain off any excess fat. Repeat with the other chicken pieces.

3. Put a large saucepan on the stove to heat and add the remaining vegetable oil. As soon it starts to smoke, add the onions, apple, garlic, ginger and peppers. Cook for about 5 minutes over a high heat, stirring all the time. Stir in the tomato purée and cook for a further 2 minutes. Add the cumin and both the curry powders or pastes. Stir the ingredients regularly so that they do not catch or burn. Add the cinnamon stick. Pour in the coconut milk and bring to the boil, stirring as you do so. Add the mango chutney. Pour in the chicken stock and bring the sauce back up to the boil. With a ladle, skim off any surfacing scum or foam and discard. Add the chicken pieces and cover the saucepan with a lid. Put it in the oven and cook for 20 minutes. Remove the curry from the oven. Give it a stir, add the potatoes, and return to the oven for a further 30 minutes. Remove the curry from the oven and serve.

Smooth Chicken and Duck Pâté

I have included this recipe because it is ideal if you are throwing a large dinner party. It's both simple to make and to serve. If you are feeling rich, add 250 g of fresh foie gras and use only 250 g of chicken livers. Some unscrupulous chefs put a teaspoon of saltpetre in the mixture to keep the pâté a beautiful pink colour. I wouldn't dream of doing that! When working with livers, always check them carefully and cut out any green gall that may be present. This must be removed or the pâté will be ruined. Once the pâté is made, keep it in the refrigerator for at least three days before cutting so that the flavours can mature. Always use a hot knife when slicing to achieve a clean cut, and cut off the pork fat around each slice. I like to serve it with a little yellow frisée (curly endive) mixed with some corn salad bound in a Walnut Oil Vinaigrette (see page 219), a slice of toast and perhaps a spoonful of pear chutney or some Cumberland Sauce (see page 217).

Serves 12–14 as a starter

500 g fresh chicken livers

250 g fresh duck livers

3 garlic cloves

3 large eggs

250 g melted unsalted butter, cooled

2 dessertspoons brandy

1 dessertspoon ruby port

salt and freshly milled black pepper

20 thin slices of pork fat

1. Carefully check the livers; they must be a fresh red colour. Cut away any green discoloration. Peel and crush the garlic cloves and put them in a liquidiser with the livers. Blitz to a smooth paste. This will take about 3 minutes. One by one, add the eggs and beat them into the mixture. Slowly add the melted butter and, whilst the machine is still running, add the brandy and then the port. Season with salt and pepper. Pour the mixture into a fine nylon sieve set over a bowl and push it through the sieve using a pastry scraper, to trap all the sinews.

2. Preheat the oven to 180°C/350°F/Gas 4.

3. Line a terrine mould (26 cm long x 7.5 cm deep x 10 cm wide) with all but one of the slices of pork fat. Overlap each piece slightly to ensure that the pâté is completely sealed. Pour the mixture into the terrine mould and lay the remaining piece of fat over the top. Cover the mould with cling film and a double layer of foil. Put in a roasting pan three-quarters filled with hot water (it should come to within 2 cm of the top), and cook for 45–55 minutes or until firm to the touch. Remove from the oven and allow to cool before refrigerating.

Potted Minced Duck

In order to mature, this dish is best kept in the refrigerator for at least two days. I like to serve it with heaps of melba toast or crunchy French bread, accompanied by a bowl of gherkins and a glass of cold Vouvray or Sancerre. A salad of mixed leaves with Walnut Oil Vinaigrette (see page 219) would complete the meal.

Serves 6 as a starter

4 large duck legs
240 g pork belly
120 g pork fat (off the loin is best)
3 garlic cloves, peeled
1 onion, chopped
1 leek, chopped
1 carrot, chopped
1 stick celery, chopped
450 ml dry white wine
1 sprig fresh thyme
1 bay leaf
6 black peppercorns, crushed
salt and freshly milled black pepper
60 g fresh parsley, finely chopped

1. Preheat the oven to 120°C/250°F/Gas ½.

2. Place the untrimmed duck legs in a large, thick-bottomed casserole with a lid. Remove the skin from the belly of pork and discard. Cut the pork into large pieces. Dice the pork fat into similar sized pieces and add them to the duck. Cover the meat with the garlic, onion, leek, carrot and celery. Pour in the wine and add the thyme, bay leaf and crushed peppercorns. Cover the dish first with foil and then a lid, place in the oven and cook for at least 4 hours or until the duck legs are tender and falling off the bone, the pork is caramelised and the wine has fully evaporated.

3. When cooked, carefully remove the duck legs, pork and fat cubes from the casserole and set aside in a bowl. Strain the vegetables, fats and meat juices through a fine sieve and then through a muslin cloth into a bowl. This liquid will be used later to top the mince. Break off all the meat and skin from the duck and discard the bones. Finely shred the meat and skin using a sharp knife. Set aside.

4. Place the pork and fat cubes in a food processor and purée. If the mixture is too thick, add some of the liquid fat and meat juices until it becomes moist. Season with a little salt and pepper. With a spatula, scrape out all of the pork and mix it with the duck, together with the parsley. Put the potted mince into a suitable earthenware dish and press it down firmly, leaving about 1 cm from the top. Smooth over the top with a spatula and place in the refrigerator for a minimum of 3 hours to set. When set, remove from the refrigerator, warm the fat and meat juices on the stove, and spoon over the potted mince to seal. Keep in the fridge, but bring to room temperature before serving.

Roasted Duck Breasts with Raspberries

This makes a delicious and fairly quick main course for a summer's evening; the only time-consuming part of this recipe is the sauce. You'll need to buy two ducks. The legs can be used for dishes such as confit of duck on a hazelnut salad. The duck carcasses and the wings are used to make the sauce. I think it's best served with mashed potatoes and a watercress and spinach salad.

Serves 4

4 x 200-g duck breasts

1 teaspoon sea salt

1 teaspoon ground cinnamon

2 teaspoons demerara sugar

1 tablespoon goose or duck fat

Duck Sauce

2 tablespoons duck or goose fat

500 g chopped duck bones

1 onion, chopped

1 carrot, peeled and chopped

1 stick celery, chopped

½ bay leaf

1 sprig thyme

2 garlic cloves, peeled and crushed

1 tablespoon redcurrant jelly

2 tablespoons raspberry vinegar

1 small glass port

1 glass red wine

200 g raspberries

250 ml Chicken Stock
    (see pages 213–14)

salt and freshly milled black pepper

50 ml Stock Syrup (see page 220)

1. First make the sauce. Place a large saucepan on the stove. Add the goose or duck fat and allow it to melt. As the fat starts to smoke, put in the chopped duck bones. Cook and colour for about 10 minutes until brown. Add the onion, carrot, celery, bay leaf, thyme and garlic. Continue frying for a further 5 minutes, just to colour the vegetables, stirring from time to time. Add the redcurrant jelly. This will glaze the bones further and they will appear sticky and syrupy. Pour in the raspberry vinegar, boil and reduce its volume by half. Add the port and boil to reduce it by half, then add the red wine and again reduce the liquid by half. Add 125 g of the raspberries and cook them to a pulp. Pour in the chicken stock and season. Bring the sauce to the boil and, with a ladle, skim off the surfacing impurities and discard. Reduce the heat to a simmer and cook the sauce for about an hour.

2. Put the sea salt, cinnamon and demerara sugar in a small bowl and mix. Sprinkle it onto a plate. Score the duck breasts through the fat with a sharp knife. Mark at least ten shallow incisions over each. Place the duck breasts, fat side down, onto the plate with the salt mixture and rub the mixture over the breasts. Set aside.

3. Pour the sauce through a fine mesh sieve set over a bowl and then pour it into another sieve lined with a piece of muslin to trap all the sediment. Pour the sauce into a saucepan and boil until its volume has been reduced by half.

4. Warm the remaining raspberries in the stock syrup and reserve.

5. Put a large frying pan on the stove to heat. Add the goose fat and, as it starts to smoke, place the duck breasts, fat side down, into the pan. Fry them for about 6 minutes to colour and melt the fat. Turn them over and cook them for a further 4 minutes. Place the breasts on a board to relax. Lay out four warm plates. Cut the duck breasts into thin horizontal slices and divide them between the four plates. Top with some raspberries and spoon some of the sauce around.

Wild Duck Terrine with Pistachio Nuts

This is my all time favourite terrine or pâté. Great for breakfast, lunch or supper; we usually have it on Boxing Day. It is best kept in the refrigerator for at least three days before using as it needs to mature. Serve with a little lamb's lettuce in a Walnut Oil Vinaigrette (see page 219) and a slice of sourdough toast. Cumberland Sauce (see page 217) is also a great accompaniment for this dish. You'll need a 1.5-litre ceramic or cast iron terrine.

Serves 12–14 as a starter

1.75-kg wild duck (dressed weight)

400 ml Chicken Stock (see pages 213–14)

2 bay leaves

2 sprigs fresh thyme

4 sprigs fresh parsley

250 g belly of pork

200 g lean pork (from the loin or leg)

250 g duck livers, cleaned and all gall removed

400 ml white wine

1 glass port

4 shallots or 1 large onion

2 garlic cloves, peeled

zest of 1 orange

salt and freshly milled black pepper

1 tablespoon sunflower oil

250 g pork fat for lining the mould, cut into thin slices

10 g butter

100 g cooked ham, diced

100 g shelled pistachio nuts

100 g pork fat, diced

1 dessertspoon green peppercorns

1. Remove the legs from the duck and carefully cut off the duck breasts. Trim off all the fat and sinew from both the legs and breasts. Cut all the meat off the bones of the legs and cut into rough pieces. Chop up the duck carcasses and the wing bones, cover them with chicken stock and bring to the boil. With a ladle, skim off all the surfacing scum and discard. Add one of the bay leaves, half the thyme and the parsley stalks, and simmer for 3 hours.

2. Remove the bones from the belly of pork and dice it into 2-cm cubes. Dice the lean pork into similar sized pieces. Place the duck leg meat, belly of pork, lean pork and duck livers into a bowl. Cover with the white wine and port, add two of the shallots, cut in half, the garlic, orange zest, the rest of the thyme and the remaining bay leaf. Cover with cling film and place in the refrigerator to marinate for at least 3 hours.

3. Season the duck breasts with salt and pepper. Add the oil to a hot frying pan and brown the duck breasts on both sides, then transfer them to a plate to cool.

4. Cut the pork fat into thin slices. (Streaky bacon can be used as an alternative). Line the mould with the slices of pork fat, overlapping each piece. Allow enough overhang at the top to seal the terrine.

5. Strain the marinated meat into a colander placed over a bowl. Remove and discard the shallots. Pour the marinade into a small saucepan and bring to the

boil. Using a small ladle, remove all the sediment that rises up to the surface and discard. Strain the duck stock through a fine sieve and pour it into the marinade. Reduce all of this liquid to a thick concentrate, which should resemble a liquid form of Marmite. Put aside to cool.

6. Chop the remaining shallots and garlic as finely as possible. Cook them in a pan with the butter until soft, but don't allow to colour. Set aside to cool.

7. Preheat the oven to 160°C/325°F/Gas 3.

8. Pass all the meats, apart from the duck breasts, through a mincer or food processor, using a fine blade, as the paté needs to be as smooth as possible. Add the diced ham, pistachio nuts, diced fat, shallots, green peppercorns and the concentrated stock. Season the mixture with salt and plenty of pepper. Put half the paté mixture into the lined terrine, pushing it down firmly to ensure that there is no air at the corners. Lay the duck breasts on top, one behind the other, making sure that they don't touch the sides of the mould. Cover the duck breasts with the remaining mixture and push it down again. Bring up the overhanging pieces of pork fat to cover the top of the terrine. Place the remaining bay leaf on top and cover the terrine with cling film to seal. Finally wrap the terrine in foil and place in a large roasting tray filled with sufficient boiling water to reach to about 4 cm from the top. Put the terrine in the oven to cook for about 1 hour and 20 minutes.

9. Remove the roasting tray from the oven. Take out the terrine, and allow to cool. Place a heavy weight on top, and leave overnight in the refrigerator. Keep in the refrigerator until ready to use. To serve, take out of the mould and slice it into portions roughly 1.5 cm thick.

Pigeon and Parma Ham Salad

I love pigeon and it is cheap. If you like shooting, it is one of the hardest game birds to hit. I'm afraid neither Kim nor the children share my enthusiasm for such hobbies. You can use streaky bacon for this dish instead of the Parma ham – and I tell you something, the bacon in Devon is fantastic!

Serves 4

2 wood pigeons

2 heads chicory

30 g caster sugar

salt and freshly milled black pepper

40 g pine kernels

80 g rocket leaves

100 ml Tarragon Vinaigrette
    (see page 219)

80 g watercress

10 ml olive oil

6 slices Parma ham, cut into 1-cm
    strips (lardons)

1. Using a very sharp knife, carefully remove the pigeon breasts from the bone. Pull off the skin and trim off any sinew and fat.

2. Cut the chicory heads in half lengthways and sprinkle them with the caster sugar, salt and pepper.

3. Preheat the oven to 230°C/450°F/Gas 8. Toast the pine kernels on a baking sheet in the oven for about 5 minutes. Be careful not to burn them.

4. Blitz half the rocket leaves with half the vinaigrette in the blender until smooth.

5. Season the pigeon breasts with salt and pepper. Put a small cast iron pan on the stove to heat. Add 5 ml of the olive oil and quickly add the breasts. Cook to brown them only, and then place them in the oven for 4–5 minutes. Remove from the oven and place on a board to relax for about 5 minutes.

6. Put the lardons of Parma ham onto a baking sheet and grill them until crisp.

7. Heat a small, metal-handled frying pan on the stove. Add the remaining olive oil and place the chicory in the pan. Cook for about 2 minutes on each side or until golden brown. Lay out four large plates. Place one of the chicory halves in the centre of each. Toss the rest of the rocket leaves, the watercress and pine kernels together in the remaining vinaigrette. Place the salad on top of the chicory. Slice the warm pigeon breasts at an angle into three pieces and place them around the salad. Spoon a little of the rocket dressing around the outside of the plate and top the salad with the grilled Parma ham.

Quail Salad with Bacon

This salad is a complete meal. I like to eat it for lunch with a glass of Chablis.

Serves 4

6 rashers of green streaky bacon, cut
    into 5-mm strips
1 French stick or baguette
3 tablespoons olive oil
1 garlic clove
4 quails, wishbones removed
salt and freshly milled black pepper
20 button mushrooms, cut in half
50 g mixed salad leaves
2 tablespoons Walnut Oil Vinaigrette
    (see page 219)
unsalted butter
4 quails' eggs
sherry vinegar

1. Preheat the oven to 200°C/400°F/Gas 6.

2. Put a small pan half filled with water on the stove to boil. When the water is boiling, add the bacon, bring back to the boil, and immediately strain through a fine sieve. Set aside. This process will remove most of the salt and impurities.

3. Cut 16 thin slices (croutons) from the French stick and place them on a baking tray. Sprinkle with a tablespoon of olive oil and bake in the oven for about 5 minutes until golden brown. Peel the garlic clove and cut it in half. Score the garlic, making several shallow incisions in the flesh to release the oil and rub it over the croutons. Set aside.

4. Season the quails with salt and pepper. Heat up a small, metal-handled frying pan. Add a tablespoon of olive oil and, as soon as it starts to smoke, add the quails and fry until golden brown on all sides, then place in the oven for 7 minutes or until pink. When cool enough to handle, carefully cut off the legs and, following the breast line with your knife, remove the breasts. Set aside but keep warm.

5. Heat the remaining tablespoon of olive oil in a frying pan. Quickly brown the bacon lardons, then add the mushrooms and allow to colour.

6. Put the salad leaves in a bowl and toss them with the walnut vinaigrette. Lay a mound of salad in the centre of each plate and place the quail around it. Spoon the bacon and mushrooms around the outside of the quail.

7. Put a small pan on the stove and add a little butter. When melted, crack in the quails' eggs and fry them until they are just set. Sprinkle over a little sherry vinegar. With a small palette knife, remove the quails' eggs and place them on four of the croutons. Top each salad with an egg crouton and place the remaining croutons around the plate.

Roast Pheasant and Cep Mushrooms

Ceps do grow in England but, as in France, they are not easy to find. Put them with a pheasant, though, and you've got a great autumn dish. You usually have to buy a brace of pheasant, i.e. a male and female, but, if you can, just buy hens, as they are much more tender. Serve with a Potato Cake (see page 134) and some spinach or buttered cabbage and bacon.

Serves 8

2 x 1.25-kg pheasants
salt and freshly milled black pepper
60 g unsalted butter, softened
1 kg fresh ceps
35 ml groundnut oil
1 onion, chopped
1 carrot, chopped
1 stick celery, chopped
1 leek, chopped
2 garlic cloves, peeled and chopped
1 sprig fresh thyme
1 sprig tarragon
½ bay leaf
1 glass port
1 glass dry white wine
400 ml Chicken Stock
    (see pages 213–14)
100 ml double cream
juice of ¼ lemon
30 g unsalted butter
2 shallots, finely diced
2 sprigs flat-leaf parsley, finely
    chopped

1. Preheat the oven to 200°C/400°F/Gas 6.

2. Season the pheasants with salt and pepper and place them in a roasting tray. Smear them with the softened butter, then place in the oven to cook for about 40 minutes.

3. Wash the ceps in lukewarm water. Strain them and, with a small knife, scrape out the gills and discard. Cut off the stalks 1 cm below the tops and wrap them in kitchen paper to dry thoroughly. Put to one side for the sauce.

4. Remove the pheasants from the oven; they should still be slightly pink. Place them on a board to relax for at least 10 minutes. Cut off the legs and remove the breasts. Place them on a serving dish and cover with foil. Set aside. Chop up the pheasant carcasses and put them back into the roasting tray. Heat the roasting tray on top of the stove, then transfer it to the oven for about 5 minutes to brown the carcasses.

5. Heat a large saucepan on the stove. Pour in the groundnut oil and, as soon as it starts to smoke, add the onion, carrot, celery and leek and fry until golden brown. Add the cep stalks, garlic, thyme, tarragon and bay leaf and cook for a couple of minutes, stirring from time to time. Pour in the port, bring to the boil, and continue to boil until it has been reduced to a syrup.

6. Remove the pheasant carcasses from the oven and put in a colander set over a bowl to trap the fats. Add the bones to the saucepan and stir them

into the sauce base. Add the white wine and continue to boil until its volume has been reduced by half. Pour in the chicken stock and return to the boil. With a ladle, skim off all the surfacing sediment and discard. Lower the heat and simmer for about 30 minutes. Strain the sauce through a fine sieve, lined with a muslin cloth, into another saucepan. Put back on the heat, bring to the boil, and reduce the sauce until it is thick enough to coat the back of a spoon. Stir in the double cream and squeeze in the lemon juice to reduce the sweetness. Season with salt and pepper.

7. Lower the oven temperature to 180°C/350°F/Gas 4, and put the pheasant back in for about 10 minutes to reheat.

8. Put a large frying pan on the stove to heat. Add the butter and, as soon as it has melted, add both the shallots and the ceps. Season with salt and pepper and fry for about 5 minutes. Pour the sauce over them and bring it to the boil.

9. Remove the pheasant from the oven, very carefully pour off any excess fat, then spoon over the sauce and sprinkle with the parsley. Serve immediately.

Roast Partridge with Barley and Parsnip Chips

Partridge is a very good way of introducing people to game. It is a white meat with a very sweet, delicate flavour and, as long as it is not hung too long, it isn't too 'gamey'. I love the texture of pearl barley in the sauce. You can substitute thinly sliced celeriac chips, or even carrot ones, for the parsnip if you prefer.

Serves 4

4 partridges, wishbone removed
salt and freshly milled black pepper
500 ml sunflower oil
40 g unsalted butter
1 onion, chopped
2 garlic cloves, chopped
250 g pearl barley
100 ml white wine
870 ml Chicken Stock
   (see pages 213–14)
1 tablespoon parsley, chopped
1 large parsnip, peeled and cut
   lengthways into fine strips

1. Preheat the oven to 200°C/400°F/Gas 6.

2. Season the partridge with salt and pepper. Heat a roasting tray on the stove. Add a tablespoon of sunflower oil and, as soon it starts to smoke, add the partridges to the pan. Colour the birds all over to seal, then place them in the oven to cook for 15 minutes.

3. Melt 25 g of the butter in a saucepan. Add the onion and garlic and gently cook for about 5 minutes or until soft. Add the pearl barley and stir it into the onion mixture until the butter is absorbed. Pour in the wine and, stirring occasionally, cook the pearly barley until the wine has totally evaporated. Add 750 ml of chicken stock and gently simmer until the pearl barley is cooked or tender. Season with a little salt and pepper. Add the parsley and keep warm on one side.

4. Remove the partridges from the oven and let them rest for 5 minutes. Pour the remaining chicken stock into a small pan and boil to reduce it by two thirds. Cut off the legs from the partridges and carefully remove the breasts. Place the legs back in the pan, flesh side down, and the breasts skin side down. Dot them with a little butter and cover with foil.

5. Fry the parsnip strips in the remaining sunflower oil until crisp and golden.

6. Reheat the partridge in the oven for about 4 minutes. Lay out four hot plates. Spoon the pearl barley into the centre of each plate. Place the partridge legs, criss-crossed, onto the barley. Lay the breasts on top of the legs. Spoon a little of the reduced chicken stock or glaze around the edge of the plates. It should be dark and sticky in texture. Place a few fried parsnip chips on top of the dish and serve immediately.

4. Meat

The lush green fields and red iron-rich soil of the Devon countryside make for fantastic pastureland and sublime meat. This beautiful county has a long tradition of rearing beef cattle, in particular, and was once home to one of the most famous and ancient breeds of all: the Red Devons, or North Devons, known locally as 'Red Rubies' because of their rich red colouring, which were taken to America by the Pilgrim Fathers in the 17th century. Although Red Rubies still graze on Exmoor, they have now largely been replaced by another breed of red cattle, the South Devons. I have been very impressed by the wide range of organic and specialist butchers I've found everywhere here. There's even a butcher in Kingsbridge, where I live, who sells beef from his own herd – a cross between the South Devon and Aberdeen Angus. It goes down a treat at home.

Devon lamb is another success story. The combination of mild winters, which allow longer grazing periods, and the

Devon is blessed with rich soil and mild winters – a winning combination that results in lush meadows and pastureland in which sheep and cattle graze freely. The results are some of the best meat I've ever tasted, and beautiful views of animals in wonderfully green fields! Many local farmers specialise in rare breeds of sheep, pigs and cattle.

rotation of rich grazing land, leads not only to healthy animals, but also to tender, succulent meat, which, along with Welsh lamb, is, in my opinion, the best the UK has to offer. In fact, when it comes to meat, it's the same story everywhere I go in the South Hams: traditional farming methods, organic rearing and local meat, all produced to the most exacting standards. This is even the case with pork, which, I must admit, I had never particularly associated with Devon, but I've been delighted with the quality of the meat, especially the bacon, which is traditionally dry cured, rather than being preserved in a brine solution. It's quite simply the best I've had anywhere.

Meat is popular big-time at home. Kim and Olivia love lamb, while Charles's favourite is roast pork – he really goes for the crackling. But all the children love beef, whether it's steak or roast beef served with Yorkshire pudding – another Sunday lunchtime favourite that always almost causes a punch-up! Martha loves my gravy so much that she drinks it by the cupful until it makes her feel sick.

Beef, pork and lamb are our staples at The New Angel, though we also have venison from Dartmoor and Exmoor, and rabbits locally caught by 'lamping', a traditional night-time method of hunting using lamps attached to rifles to pick them out. But I don't tell Eliza and Amelia that!

Rib of Beef with Red Wine and Marrow Sauce

Make sure that the beef you choose has some fatty marbling through the eye of the meat and that it has been hung for at least ten days. French beans and some deep-fried new potatoes in their skins go well with this one.

Serves 8

2 x 1-kg rib of beef on the bone

2 tablespoons groundnut oil

coarsely ground sea salt and freshly milled black pepper

1 bunch watercress

Beef Marrow

12 large slices of beef marrow, soaked overnight in cold, salted water in the refrigerator

4 shallots or 1 red onion, finely chopped

75 ml red wine vinegar

salt and freshly milled black pepper

Red Wine Sauce

75 g unsalted butter

6 shallots or 1 red onion, finely chopped (try and use shallots where possible)

1 clove garlic, peeled and chopped

½ bay leaf

1 sprig thyme

1 sprig tarragon

300 g plain flour

500 ml red wine

250 ml Beef Stock (see page 215)

1. First make the sauce. Melt the butter in a saucepan, add the shallots and fry until golden brown. Add the garlic, bay leaf, thyme and tarragon. Add the flour and stir. Cook for about 2 minutes, then pour in the wine, stirring all the time. Bring to the boil and reduce the liquid by two thirds. Add the beef stock and bring it back to the boil. With a ladle, skim off all the surfacing sediment and discard. Reduce the heat and cook for a further 30 minutes, reducing the volume by half.

2. Next cook the beef marrow. Half-fill a small pan with water and bring to a simmer on the stove. Remove the marrow bones from the refrigerator and place in the water to poach for about 6 minutes. Drain the water and put to one side.

3. Put the shallots in a bowl, pour over the red wine vinegar and season. Set aside.

4. Place a heavy-bottomed frying pan on the stove on a high heat and turn the grill on full.

5. Place the ribs of beef onto a tray and add half the groundnut oil. Season with sea salt and black pepper. Turn them over and rub in the oil. Heat the remaining oil in the frying pan and place the beef on it. Fry for about 4 minutes on each side for rare, and for about 7 minutes for medium.

6. Strain the sauce into another saucepan and bring it to the boil. Pour the sauce into a sauce boat.

7. Remove the ribs of beef from the frying pan, place them on a baking tray and top with the beef marrow. Warm under the grill for about 1 minute, then place on a carving board. Sprinkle the red wine vinegar and shallots over the marrow.

Roast Beef and Yorkshire Puddings

Maybe it's because I'm British, but, personally, I don't think you can beat a traditional roast beef for a Sunday lunch. My favourite is rib of beef since, as with most large joints, it always tastes better on the bone. When choosing the beef, ask your butcher to give you the bones from chining the beef or any others that are available. This will give you a good gravy and lift the beef off the bottom of the tray, ensuring that it doesn't burn on one side. The children fight over my Yorkshire puddings, so I've given up making little individual ones and instead cook a big one in a large roasting tray – Martha always gets my piece! I love horseradish sauce with roast beef. Roast potatoes are essential. You could also serve some Glazed Carrots (see page 142), broccoli and French beans.

Serves 8

1 x 3-kg forerib of beef (3 ribs)
salt and freshly milled black pepper
3 tablespoons beef dripping or lard
beef bones from chining the joint,
   chopped

Yorkshire Pudding
225 g plain flour
½ teaspoon salt
3 eggs
350 ml milk
4 tablespoons dripping
1 teaspoon malt vinegar
salt and freshly milled black pepper

Gravy
1 large onion, chopped
1 large carrot, peeled and chopped
1 stick celery, chopped
½ bay leaf
1 sprig thyme
300 ml Beef/Veal Stock (see page 215)
1 teaspoon cornflour or arrowroot
salt and freshly milled black pepper

1. Preheat the oven to 200°C/400°F/Gas 6.

2. Season the meat with salt and lots of pepper. Heat the dripping or lard in a large roasting tray on the stove and, as soon as it starts to smoke, carefully place the beef joint in the roasting tray and seal it on all sides until brown (about 3 minutes per side). Lift out the beef and add the chopped beef bones. Put the beef on top of the bones and place in the oven. Allow about 15 minutes per 450 g for medium rare. Every so often, baste the meat with the juices and fat from the bottom of the tray.

3. For the Yorkshire pudding batter, increase the oven temperature to 220°C/425°F/Gas 7. Sieve the flour into a large bowl. Add the salt. Crack the eggs into the flour and, with a whisk, beat in the milk. Continue whisking the batter until it becomes smooth. Melt a tablespoon of the dripping on the stove and, as soon as it has melted, stir it into the batter. Add the vinegar and season with salt and pepper. Strain the batter through a fine sieve into a clean glass bowl and place in the refrigerator to relax for at least 20 minutes.

4. Place a roasting pan on the stove with 3 tablespoons of dripping and heat it until it starts to smoke. Remove the Yorkshire pudding batter from the refrigerator and whisk it until smooth. Pour it into the hot dripping and place it in the oven to cook for about 40 minutes.

5. When the beef is cooked, remove from the oven and transfer to a board to rest. Pour off the fat from the roasting pan. Place the pan on the stove over a high heat and add the onion, carrot, celery, bay leaf and thyme, and cook with the bones to colour. Stir continuously until the vegetables are brown. Pour in the beef/veal stock and bring the gravy to the boil. With a ladle, skim off all the surfacing sediment and discard. Reduce the heat to a gentle simmer.

6. Mix the cornflour or arrowroot with 3 tablespoons of cold water and stir it into the gravy to thicken. Strain the gravy through a fine sieve over a saucepan. Discard the bones. Season with salt and pepper and continue to simmer gently.

7. With a sharp knife, cut away the three rib bones and carve the meat into slices. Serve two slices of meat per person. Ladle a little gravy around the meat. Remove the Yorkshire

pudding from the oven and cut it into eight. Place the pudding on the plates and serve immediately.

Charles's Beef Tea

I like cars, shooting and fishing. If you participate in any of these pursuits, they usually require an early start and, invariably, cold, wet and sometimes atrocious weather conditions. Fill your thermos flask with this, drink a few cups spiked with alcohol, and the whole world looks like a better place, especially when you can't feel your fingers or toes in the winter months! Charles, unbeknown to Kim, prefers his with vodka! I think beef tea is a better drink than hot mulled wine, if, of course, you're not a vegetarian! Make it the night before you go out. You will need a good manual mincer with a fine cutting blade or an electric one attached to a Kenwood Chef or similar machine. It will keep for up to three days in the refrigerator.

Makes 2 litres

1.5 kg shin, flank or chuck beef (use
    only the cheaper cuts for this dish)
2 garlic cloves, peeled
1 onion, roughly chopped
1 carrot, cut in half
2 sticks celery
2 sprigs flat-leaf parsley
1 sprig fresh thyme
1 bay leaf
3–4 drops Worcestershire sauce
2–3 drops Tabasco
salt and freshly milled black pepper
100 g tomato purée
5–6 egg whites
2 litres cold water

1. Cut the meat into small pieces and mince into a large saucepan. Peel and roughly chop the garlic, onion, carrot and celery and mince in the same way. Add the parsley, thyme, bay leaf, Worcestershire sauce, Tabasco and salt and pepper, and stir until well mixed. Finally, stir in the tomato purée.

2.Pour the egg whites over the minced beef and mix thoroughly with your hands. Add the water and place the pan on the stove to cook over a high heat. Stir continuously for about 10 minutes until the beef tea starts to boil. As the liquid comes up to the boil a crust will rise to the surface. As soon as it is boiling underneath the crust, stop stirring and quickly reduce the heat to a gentle simmer. Simmer for 2 hours.

3. Remove the pan from the stove and make a little hole in the crust just big enough to insert a ladle. Ladle the tea into a sieve lined with a muslin cloth set over a bowl. Discard all of the crust. Allow the beef tea to cool, then cover it with cling film and refrigerate. Boil the beef tea in the morning and put it into your thermos flask. Don't forget the vodka!

Spaghetti Bolognese

The kids love this dish and it is always a favourite with their friends. Serve the spaghetti tossed in a little olive oil with hot garlic bread on the side. This is another dish that tastes better reheated the next day. Use any leftover meat sauce to make a lasagne – just add White Sauce (page 216), cheese and pasta.

Serves 8

3 tablespoons olive oil

2 onions, diced

3 garlic cloves, finely chopped

1 sprig rosemary

2 sprigs thyme

1 bay leaf

1 kg lean minced beef (not too finely ground)

140 g tomato purée

5 tomatoes, skinned, seeded and diced

150 g button mushrooms

1 glass red wine

300 ml Beef Stock (see page 215)

salt and freshly milled black pepper

1. Heat the olive oil in a large lidded saucepan. As soon as it starts to smoke, add the onions, then the garlic, and stir. Fry until softened but not coloured.

2. Add the rosemary, thyme and bay leaf, and the minced beef. Cook to colour the beef over a very high heat for at least 10 minutes. Stir in the tomato purée and cook for a further 5 minutes.

3. Add the diced tomatoes and the mushrooms. Stir in the red wine and boil until its volume has been reduced by half. Pour in the beef stock and bring to the boil, stirring. Season with salt and lots of pepper. Lower the heat to a moderate simmer and cover with a lid. The meat sauce will take about half an hour to cook. During this time stir it occasionally to make sure that it doesn't catch or burn on the bottom of the pan.

Sirloin Steaks with Spicy Butter

This delicious dish works well with beef but you could also serve the spicy butter with grilled lobsters and langoustines as a tasty variation.

Serves 6

6 x 200-g sirloin steaks
salt and freshly milled black pepper
2 tablespoons groundnut oil or
    dripping

Spicy Butter

250 g unsalted butter, cut into small
    pieces
1 sprig thyme
½ bay leaf
1 sprig fresh tarragon
2 shallots or 1 small onion, finely
    chopped
1 garlic clove, peeled and finely
    chopped
30 ml white wine
1 teaspoon Madras curry paste or
    powder
30 g parsley, finely chopped
1 teaspoon capers, chopped
3 small gherkins, chopped
3 anchovy fillets, chopped
2 large egg yolks
1 pinch cayenne pepper
juice of ¼ lemon
salt and freshly milled black pepper

1. First make the sauce. Put the butter in the bowl of a food processor and beat it until soft and almost white in colour. Pick the leaves from the thyme stalks and finely chop, along with the bay leaf. Pick the leaves from the tarragon stalks and blanch them in boiling water for 10 seconds. Refresh in cold water and strain through a sieve. Dry the leaves on some kitchen paper and finely chop.

2. Melt a spoonful of the softened butter in a frying pan. Add the shallots and garlic and fry for about 5 minutes but do not colour. Add the white wine and boil until it has evaporated completely. Stir in the curry paste and cook for a further 2 minutes. Add the thyme and chopped bay leaf, then remove the pan from the heat to cool.

3. Add the parsley, capers, gherkins, anchovies and tarragon to the remaining butter in the food processor. Beat the ingredients together until well mixed and then, one at a time, add the egg yolks, followed by the cayenne pepper and lemon juice. Season with a little salt and pepper and add the shallot mixture. Beat the ingredients together. Transfer to a bowl using a spatula.

4. Turn the grill on full and put a large frying pan onto the stove to heat. Add the oil or dripping. Season the steaks with salt and lots of pepper. When the oil starts to smoke, put the steaks in the frying pan and cook for 2 minutes on each side. Remove from the pan and place on a baking sheet. Top each steak with a tablespoon of the spicy butter and put under the grill to glaze. The butter will start to melt and turn golden. Serve with some chips and a side salad and, possibly, a little red wine sauce.

Steak and Kidney Pie

You can make the filling for this dish one or two days ahead, if you like. Shortcrust pastry can be substituted for puff pastry. If you have saved and frozen a lot of puff pastry trimmings in the past use these; it doesn't have to be virgin pastry. Serve with a green vegetable and some Glazed Carrots (see page 142).

Serves 8–10

750 g lean beef chuck or topside,
    diced into 3-cm cubes
300 g lambs' kidneys (out of their fat),
    diced into 2-cm cubes
4 tablespoons lard or beef dripping
1 large carrot, diced into 1-cm cubes
2 onions, diced into 1-cm cubes
1 stick celery, diced into 1-cm cubes
1 large leek, split, diced into
    1-cm cubes
100 g tomato purée
200 g button mushrooms
350 ml red wine
1 bay leaf
1 sprig thyme
600 ml Beef/Veal Stock (see page 215)
1 teaspoon Worcestershire sauce
salt and freshly milled black pepper
350 g Shortcrust Pastry (see page 213)
1 egg, beaten until smooth
flour, for dusting

Variation

You can use venison instead of beef, if you prefer, in which case use veal kidneys rather than lambs' kidneys. You can also use veal kidneys with beef if you find the flavour of lamb too strong.

1. Heat half the lard or dripping in a large frying pan and, as soon as it starts to smoke, add the diced beef and fry to colour it brown. It's best to do this in two batches, which will take about 7 minutes. Remove the beef from the pan with a slotted spoon and set aside in a bowl. Seal the diced lambs' kidneys in the same pan, then put with the beef.

2. Heat the remaining lard or beef dripping in a large lidded saucepan or casserole. When hot, add the carrot, onions, celery and leek and fry to a golden colour. Add the tomato purée and cook for 2 minutes before adding the mushrooms. Pour in the red wine and boil until it has been reduced by half. Add the bay leaf and thyme. Pour in the beef/veal stock and bring it to the boil. With a ladle, skim off all the surfacing sediment. Add the Worcestershire sauce and seasoning. Add the beef and kidneys and lower the heat to a gentle simmer. Cover with the lid and cook for about 1 hour 15 minutes or until the meat is tender. Transfer the filling to a pie dish to cool.

3. Preheat the oven to 190°C/375°F/Gas 5.

4. On a lightly floured surface, roll out the pastry to a thickness of about 7. 5 mm; you will need a piece large enough to cover the pie. Using a pastry brush, brush around the inner edge of the pie dish with the beaten egg. Carefully lay the pastry on top of the filling. Press down onto the edge of the pie dish and, using your forefinger and thumb, crimp the edges. With a sharp knife, cut away any excess, pastry. Brush the top of the pie with some more egg wash and place the pie in the refrigerator to rest for 20 minutes, then cook for about 40 minutes. The pastry should be golden and the pie filling hot.

Braised Lamb Shanks

This makes an excellent and inexpensive dish to serve on a cold, gusty autumn evening. I like to serve a green vegetable – maybe some quickly fried baby spinach leaves or some green beans – and Jerusalem Artichoke Mash (see page 142) with this dish. The mash cuts through the rich wine sauce perfectly. Take my advice and don't serve a starter beforehand. Follow with a fruit dessert. Try the Pink Grapefruit Ice (see page 179).

Serves 6

6 lamb shanks, each weighing about
   600g, including the bone
salt and freshly milled black pepper
3 tablespoons olive oil
1 large onion, roughly chopped
2 cloves garlic, crushed
1 large carrot, roughly chopped
2 sticks celery, chopped
1 leek, chopped
1 sprig thyme
1 sprig rosemary
1 bay leaf
1 tablespoon tomato purée
1 heaped tablespoon plain flour
350 ml dry white wine
1 litre Lamb Stock (see pages 214–15)

1. Preheat the oven to 160°C/325°F/Gas 3.

2. Season the lamb shanks. Place a large lidded casserole or roasting tin on the stove over a high heat. Add 2 tablespoons of olive oil and, as soon as the oil starts to smoke, seal the shanks all over until they are a good brown colour. This will take about 10 minutes.

3. Remove the lamb shanks to a board. Add the remaining tablespoon of olive oil to the pan, then add the onion, garlic, carrot, celery and leek and fry until brown in colour. Add the thyme, rosemary and bay leaf. Stir in the tomato purée and the flour. Cook for a further 3–4 minutes. Pour in the wine and stir the sauce base until smooth. Bring to the boil and reduce by half. Put the lamb back into the pan and pour in the lamb stock. Bring to the boil, cover with a lid and place in the oven for approximately 2½ hours or until the lamb is tender.

4. Remove the lamb shanks from the oven and place them on a tray. Strain the stock through a fine sieve into a saucepan. Boil and reduce the stock by half or until it thickens. The lamb shanks can be kept warm over the stove or in a warm oven.

5. Serve the lamb shanks with the sauce poured over the top.

Blackawton Lamb with Crushed Peas, Mint and Tomato Sauce

The only time to buy lamb is in the spring and early summer, after that it becomes too strong in flavour. For most meat sauce cookery, it is usually necessary to caramelise and colour the bones to achieve a brownish sauce. In this dish what I am looking for is a red sauce – the colour of tomatoes – so the preparation is completely different. I like to serve it with a Fondant Potatoes (see page 137) between the peas.

Serves 4

2 x 6-bone best end of lamb
500 g lamb bones, trimmed of all fat
    and chopped small
500 ml Chicken Stock
    (see pages 213–14)
1 onion, chopped
½ large carrot, peeled and chopped
1 leek, chopped
1 stick celery, chopped
4 cloves garlic
1 sprig thyme
1 bay leaf
salt and freshly milled black pepper
1 tablespoon sunflower oil
30 g unsalted butter
2 shallots, roughly chopped
250 g fresh, ripe tomatoes, roughly
    chopped
50 g tomato purée
150 g fresh peas, shelled
150 g frozen peas
3 sprigs mint

1. Place the lamb bones in a saucepan and cover with cold water. Bring to the boil and, with a ladle, skim off all the surfacing sediment and discard. Drain the bones through a colander and place in another pan. Cover with the chicken stock, put back on the stove and bring to the boil. With a ladle, again skim off any surfacing sediment and discard. Reduce the heat to a moderate simmer. Add the onion, carrot, leek, celery, two of the garlic cloves, peeled and crushed, and the thyme and bay leaf and cook for about 1 hour 30 minutes.

2. Preheat the oven to 220°C/425°F/Gas 7.

3. Season the lamb with salt and pepper. Place a large frying pan on the stove to heat, add the sunflower oil and, as soon as it starts to smoke, seal the lamb on all sides. Transfer to a roasting tray and cook them in the oven for about 20 minutes. When they are cooked but still pink put them to one side to relax, but keep warm.

4. Strain the lamb stock through a colander into another saucepan. Bring to the boil and, with a ladle, again skim off any surfacing sediment and discard. Continue to boil until the volume of the stock has been reduced by half.

5. Melt half the butter in a frying pan, add the shallots and cook until softened. Be careful not to colour them. Peel the remaining garlic cloves and add to the shallots. Cut up the tomatoes, squeeze out the seeds and discard. Chop up the flesh and add it to the shallots, along with the tomato purée, and cook for about 10 minutes. Add the tomato base to the reducing stock. It will instantly take on a reddish colour. Continue cooking for a further 5 minutes, then strain the sauce through a fine sieve into another pan. Keep warm.

6. Place a large saucepan, half filled with water, on the stove to boil. When it boils, add the fresh peas and cook until tender. Add the frozen peas and, the moment they come to the boil, strain through a colander, then cool in a sink of cold water, making sure to leave them in the colander. Strain again. In a liquidiser, blitz the peas to a pulp. Season with salt and pepper and some chopped or shredded mint. Melt the remaining butter in a small frying pan and add the crushed peas. Stir from time to time.

7. Reheat the lamb in the oven. Lay out four hot serving plates and spoon a puddle of the tomato sauce in the centre of each. Take the lamb out of the oven. Cut the best ends into 12 cutlets and arrange them, supporting each other, standing up on the plates. Take 2 dessertspoons and mould two egg-shaped portions of the peas for each plate. Serve immediately.

Grilled Lamb Kebabs

This is one for the barbecue. You will need to marinate the meat for 24 hours. The kebabs are great with Cucumber, Mint and Yoghurt Salad (see page 131) and some saffron-flavoured rice.

Serves 4

1-kg leg of lamb
1 red pepper
1 yellow pepper
1 courgette
freshly milled black pepper
6 bay leaves

Marinade

4 garlic cloves, crushed
2 teaspoons cumin seeds, crushed
2 teaspoons sweet paprika
1 sprig fresh coriander, chopped
juice of 1 lemon
1 pinch saffron infused with
    2 tablespoons boiling water
½ onion, diced
200 ml full-fat natural yoghurt

1. Dice the lamb into 3-cm squares with no fat or gristle or ask your butcher to do it for you. Cut each pepper in half lengthways and remove the seeds. Cut in half again and then into 3-cm squares. Cut the courgette into 1-cm slices. Put the lamb in a mixing bowl, add the peppers and courgette, and season with pepper.

2. Thread the meat and vegetables onto the skewers, alternating first red pepper, then courgette, then yellow pepper, starting and finishing with meat, and remembering to use a bay leaf on each kebab.

3. Put all the ingredients for the marinade into a separate bowl and mix together. Place the kebabs in a flat dish or high-sided tray and cover them with the marinade. Turn the kebabs over to ensure that they are completely coated. Cover with cling film and refrigerate for 24 hours.

4. When the barbecue is hot, remove the kebabs from the refrigerator and lift them out of the marinade. Lay the kebabs on the barbecue and cook for about 20 minutes (exactly how long will depend on your barbecue), turning often. Serve.

Leg of Lamb in Salt Crust

I like to serve this with Glazed Carrots and a Potato Cake (see pages 142 and 134).

Serves 6

2-kg leg of lamb
salt and freshly milled black pepper
1 tablespoon French mustard

Sauce

1 kg lamb bones chopped small
60 ml olive oil
1 onion, roughly chopped
1 carrot, chopped
1 stick celery, chopped
1 leek, white part only, chopped
2 large ripe tomatoes, seeded
30 g tomato purée
2 garlic cloves, peeled and chopped
1 sprig thyme
½ bay leaf
1 glass white wine
1 litre Chicken Stock (see pages 213–14)
lemon juice

Salt Crust

550 g plain flour
225 g table salt
1 teaspoon fresh thyme leaves
150 ml egg whites
110 ml water
1 egg, beaten until smooth

Parsley Breadcrumbs

90 g fresh white breadcrumbs
90 g parsley
1 sprig fresh thyme
½ bay leaf
3 garlic cloves, peeled and crushed
60 ml olive oil
salt and freshly milled black pepper

1. Season the leg of lamb with salt and lots of pepper, then seal it in a very hot pan. This takes about 10 minutes.

2. Using a pastry brush, brush over all the leg with mustard. This will help the breadcrumbs to stick. Put aside in the refrigerator.

3. Preheat the oven to 200°C/400°F/Gas 6.

4. Place the lamb bones in a roasting tray and put them in the oven to brown.

5. Heat a large saucepan on the stove. Add the olive oil and, as soon as it starts to smoke, add the onion, carrot, celery and leek. Cook for about 5 minutes to colour golden brown. Add the tomatoes and tomato purée. Stir into the vegetables. Add the garlic, thyme and bay leaf. Stir again. Add the white wine and boil it until it has been reduced to a syrup. Pour in the chicken stock and bring to the boil. With a ladle, skim off any surfacing sediment and discard. Remove the bones from the oven and turn them out into a colander placed over a bowl. Add the bones to the stock, discarding the fat. Bring the sauce back to the boil, skim off the surfacing fats and discard. Reduce the heat to a simmer.

6. Next make the salt crust. Sieve the flour into the bowl of a food mixer, attach the dough hook, add the salt and the thyme. Turn the food mixer on to its lowest speed. Add the egg whites and mix for 4–5 minutes. Increase the speed a little and slowly add the water. As the paste comes together, reduce the speed and continue mixing for a further 2 minutes. You can tell when the crust is ready when it starts to come away cleanly from the sides of the bowl. Gather up all the paste from the bowl and dough hook. Dust a work surface with a little flour and roll the crust into a ball. Wrap in cling film and leave to relax for 20 minutes. You can make the pastry by hand if you prefer.

7. Put the coarsely cut breadcrumbs into a bowl and add the parsley. Pick the leaves from the thyme, crush the bay leaf and stir into the breadcrumbs, along with the garlic, mixing everything thoroughly together. Slowly add the oil, again mixing it in thoroughly, but do not over mix or the breadcrumbs will roll up into a solid ball. They should be loose, moist and bright green. Season with salt and pepper.

8. Increase the oven temperature to 230°C/450°F/Gas 8.

9. Remove the lamb from the refrigerator. Sprinkle all the breadcrumbs over the top of the lamb and press them down to stick. Unwrap the salt crust and cut in half. Dust a work surface with a little flour and roll out each piece to a thickness of 4 mm; both should be big enough to wrap the leg. Place the leg of lamb on one of the pieces of pastry. With a small pastry brush, brush a little of the beaten egg around the edge of the pastry. Bring the sides up and press them into the lamb to stick. Press the pastry into the leg bone. Brush a little more egg wash over the pastry where it meets the lamb. Carefully lay the second piece of pastry over the top of the lamb, overlapping the first piece. Press and seal the pastry together and brush the egg wash all over. Put the lamb on a baking sheet dusted with flour and cook in the oven for about 1 hour 10 minutes. After about 30 minutes reduce the oven temperature to 200°C/400°F/Gas 6 and cover the lamb with a sheet of tin foil.

10. Meanwhile, strain the sauce through a colander into a bowl, discard the bones and vegetables and pour the sauce through a fine sieve into another pan. Put the pan on the stove and bring the sauce back to the boil. With a ladle, skim off any surfacing fats and discard. Continue to boil the sauce until it has been reduced by about a third – it should have a consistency thick enough to coat the back of a spoon. Lower the heat and squeeze in a little lemon juice to take away some of the sweetness.

11. To serve, strain the sauce into a sauce boat. Remove the lamb from the oven and place it on a board. Cut down the middle of the salt crust pastry and, with a carving fork, remove the leg to another board. Discard the salt crust shell.

Slow-cooked Belly of Pork

I like to serve boiled rice with this rich dish.

Serves 6

1 kg belly pork, boned

grated zest of 1 orange

1 teaspoon cinnamon

1 teaspoon mild curry powder

salt and freshly milled black pepper

2 tablespoons sunflower oil

2 large onions, chopped

3 garlic cloves, peeled and finely
   chopped

1 teaspoon mace

¼ teaspoon cayenne pepper

1 teaspoon celery seeds

½ teaspoon salt

1 sprig each of marjoram, sage, thyme
   and rosemary

425 ml red wine

750 ml Chicken Stock
   (see pages 213–14)

115 g raisins

1 Granny Smith apple, diced

juice of 1 orange

2 teaspoons brown sugar

30 g walnuts

175 g dates

115 g dried apricots

zest and juice of 1 lemon

1. Preheat the oven to 160°C/325°F/Gas 3.

2. Lay out the belly of pork, skin side down, and season it with the grated orange zest, cinnamon and curry powder. Roll it up, tie it together with string, and sprinkle with salt and pepper.

3. Place a heavy lidded casserole on the stove to heat, add the oil and, when hot, brown the pork all over. Transfer to a plate on one side.

4. In the same casserole, fry the onions and garlic. Add the mace, cayenne pepper, celery seeds, salt, marjoram, sage, thyme and rosemary, and cook over a moderate heat for a further 2 minutes. Pour in the red wine and bring to the boil. Add the chicken stock, bring back to the boil, then reduce the heat to a simmer. Put in the pork and add the raisins, apple, orange juice, sugar and walnuts. Cover with the lid and put it in the oven for about 2 hours or until the pork is tender.

5. Put the dates, apricots and lemon juice in a small pan and cook gently over a moderate heat until the fruit is soft. Pour into a blender and blitz to form a purée. Pour this into a bowl and set aside.

6. Take the the casserole out of the oven. Carefully remove the pork from the stock and place on a serving dish. Boil the stock until its volume has been reduced by half, then stir in the apricot and date purée to thicken it still further. Cut the string off the pork and pour the sauce over it. Serve immediately.

The Kids' Sausage Rolls

You can serve these sausage rolls either hot or cold, though in our family they never get a chance to go cold!

Makes 12 (big ones)
1 kg shoulder of pork
140 g white breadcrumbs
60 g flat-leaf parsley, finely chopped
salt and freshly milled black pepper
1 egg
flour, for dusting
500 g Puff Pastry (see page 213)

1. Cut the shoulder of pork into small pieces and put in a mincer or food processor. If using a mincing machine, put the meat through twice to get a fine purée. Put the pork mince into a bowl. Add the breadcrumbs and parsley. Season with salt and pepper and, using your hands, mix everything together and roll into a ball. Refrigerate.

2. Crack the egg into a small bowl and beat it with a fork until smooth. Set aside.

3. Dust a worktop with a little flour. Cut the pastry in half and roll one piece out to a long strip 12 cm wide x 3 mm thick. Repeat.

4. Divide the sausage meat in two and roll each half into a sausage shape. Place one of the sausages just off centre in the middle of one of the halves of pastry. Brush the egg wash around the edges of the pastry, and bring the outer edge over the sausage to meet at the other edge, pressing down to seal. Shape with your hands into a roll, making sure to press out any air that may be trapped. Using a fork, crimp the edge to ensure a good seal. Cut the sausage into six and, with the back of a knife, score the tops. Brush the tops of the sausage rolls with more egg wash and put them on a baking sheet lined with greaseproof paper. Repeat for the other piece of pastry and sausage meat. Place in the refrigerator to relax for 15 minutes.

5. Preheat the oven to 220°C/425°F/Gas 7.

6. Remove the sausage rolls from the refrigerator and place in the oven to cook for 20 minutes.

Roast Loin of Pork with Prunes and Apple

The tradition of serving a fruit with fattier meats such as pork, duck or goose is not exclusive to France. At The New Angel I do a roasted loin of pork with a stuffed or baked apple with prunes for the Sunday lunch menu and I use a local Devon dry cider for the sauce – it's delicious! Get your butcher to remove the rib and chine bones and chop them up small. You will need these for the sauce. Also ask him to tie the loin for roasting. I like to eat young, buttered spinach, Glazed Carrots and Roast Potatoes (see pages 142 and 132) or mashed potatoes with this dish.

Serves 6

1.5–2-kg loin of pork
salt and freshly milled black pepper
2 tablespoons groundnut oil

Sauce

2 tablespoons groundnut oil
500 g pork bones, chopped small
1 onion, chopped
1 carrot, peeled and chopped
1 stick celery, chopped
2 garlic cloves, peeled and crushed
½ bay leaf
2 sprigs thyme
2 Granny Smith apples
200 ml dry cider
400 ml Chicken Stock
   (see pages 213–14)

Apples

5 Granny Smith apples
35 g unsalted butter
35 g soft brown sugar
12 prunes
1 pinch cinnamon
2 tablespoons Calvados or brandy
lemon juice

1. Preheat the oven to 200°C/400°F/Gas 6.

2. Rub salt into the rind of the pork to get a good crisp crackling, then season with pepper. Put a large roasting pan on the stove to heat. Add the groundnut oil and, as soon as it starts to smoke, carefully place the pork into the oil. Seal and lightly colour the pork, then place in the oven for about 1 hour 20 minutes.

3. Next make the sauce. Put a large saucepan on the stove to heat. Add the oil and, as soon as it starts to smoke, add the bones and fry them until golden brown in colour. Add the onion, carrot, celery, garlic, bay leaf and thyme and fry until coloured brown. Chop the apples, including the cores, and add them to the pan. Pour in the cider, and boil until its volume has been reduced by half or until the apples become soft. Pour in the chicken stock and bring it back to the boil. With a ladle, skim off the surfacing sediment and discard. Reduce the heat to a moderate simmer.

4. Cut three of the five Granny Smith apples in half (horizontally) and core them. Place in a buttered baking dish, cut side up, sprinkle with half the brown sugar and bake in the oven for about 10 minutes to soften.

5. Peel and core the remaining apples and coarsely grate them into a bowl. Split the prunes and remove the stones. Cut them into small strips and add them to the grated apple, together with the cinnamon, the remaining brown sugar and butter, the Calvados and a little lemon juice. Mix all the ingredients together well. Remove the par-baked apples from the oven and fill them with the prune mixture. Reduce the oven temperature to 180°C/350°F/Gas 4 and bake for a further 25 minutes. Time this with the cooking of the pork.

6. Meanwhile, strain the sauce through a fine sieve into another saucepan, then bring back up to the boil. With a ladle, skim off any surfacing sediment and discard. Continue to boil the sauce until its volume has been reduced by half.

The sauce will start to thicken as it reduces and the flavour of the apples and cider will start to come through.

7. Remove the loin of pork from the oven and place it on a serving plate or board to rest. Carefully pour off the fat from the roasting pan and place the pan on the stove. Pour in the sauce and bring it back to the boil to collect all the meat juices. Strain the sauce through another fine sieve lined with a piece of muslin cloth to trap all the sediment. Arrange the baked apples around the pork. Bring the dish to the table with the sauce served separately in a sauce boat.

Ham Hock with Broad Beans in a Parsley Sauce

My grandmother used to make this for me from time to time but she didn't peel the broad beans and it spoilt the dish. The skins of broad beans are leathery and bitter; it is worth removing them. The ham hock will need to be soaked overnight. Do not throw away any left over ham stock. Strain it into a plastic container to cool – it can then be used to make Pea and Ham Soup (see page 128) or Peas with Onion and Lettuce (see page 130). Mashed potatoes are a great accompaniment.

Serves 8

Boiled Ham

1.25-kg ham hock or bacon collar, soaked overnight
1 onion, chopped in half
1 garlic clove, peeled
1 large carrot, chopped in half
1 leek, chopped in half
1 stick celery, chopped in half
1 bay leaf
1 sprig thyme
1 teaspoon cracked black peppercorns
1 litre Chicken Stock (see pages 213–14)
1 kg broad beans, podded

Parsley Sauce

250 ml White Sauce (see page 216)
100 ml double cream
60 g finely chopped parsley
1 large sprig parsley, to garnish

1. Soak the ham joint overnight in a bowl of cold water to remove all the excess salt. Drain it and put into a large saucepan covered with water. Bring it to the boil as quickly as possible, then drain it again.

2. Add the onion, garlic carrot, leek, celery, bay leaf, thyme and peppercorns to the ham and cover with the chicken stock. Bring to the boil and, with a ladle, skim off any surfacing sediment and discard. Reduce the heat to a simmer and cook gently for about 1½ hours.

3. Put a large saucepan of water on the stove to boil. Add a large pinch of salt. When the water is boiling, add the beans and boil for 3 minutes. Strain, then refresh under cold running water. Strain again. Peel the beans and discard the skins. Put to one side in a bowl.

4. Put the white sauce in a pan and, over a gentle heat, stir it until smooth. Remove 150 ml of the ham cooking stock and whisk it into the sauce. Bring to the boil and reduce it to thicken. Add the cream. Strain the sauce through a fine sieve into another saucepan and keep it warm over a low heat. Add the broad beans, taste, and add a little seasoning if necessary. Finally, stir in the parsley.

5. Using a large fork, remove the ham from the stock and put it onto a board. Cut off the string and carefully trim off the rind. Lay the ham on a serving dish. Ladle the beans in parsley sauce around the joint. Finally, place a large sprig of parsley on top.

Samosas

These are great to serve as a hot appetiser before a meal or as nibbles for a drinks party. Alternatively, make larger ones and serve them with Mint, Cucumber and Yoghurt Salad (see page 131) for supper. I use minced leg of lamb, but you can use beef or minced chicken leg as a substitute. As with anything curried, it's always better to leave the mixture in the fridge overnight, to achieve a more mature flavour.

Makes 12

500 g lean minced lamb

vegetable oil

125 g minced or finely chopped onion, carrot, celery and leek (about 30 g of each)

4 garlic cloves, crushed

30 g Madras curry powder

30 g plain flour

30 g tomato purée

salt and freshly milled black pepper

400 ml Chicken Stock (see pages 213–14)

1 sprig thyme

1 bay leaf

1 dessertspoon redcurrant jelly

60 g green lentils, cooked until tender (puy lentils are best)

30 g freshly grated coconut or desiccated coconut

1 egg

12 sheets filo pastry

2 litres corn oil, for deep-fat frying

1. Place a large heavy-bottomed frying pan on the stove to heat. Add 4 tablespoons of cooking oil and, as soon as it starts to smoke, carefully add the minced lamb, minced vegetables and garlic. Stir and cook for about 10 minutes until coloured brown and the liquid has evaporated. Stir in the curry powder, reduce the heat slightly, and cook for about 3 minutes. Add the flour and stir vigorously. Add the tomato purée, then stir in the chicken stock, a little at a time, and bring up to the boil. Season with salt and pepper. Stir from time to time, to prevent the ingredients catching and burning on the bottom. Add the thyme, bay leaf and redcurrant jelly. Reduce the heat to a gentle simmer and cook for a further 10 minutes. Stir in the cooked lentils, add the coconut and immediately turn the mixture out onto a plastic tray. When cool, cover the mince with cling film and refrigerate, overnight if possible.

2. Beat the egg in a small bowl until smooth. Lightly dust a clean work surface with a little flour. Carefully lay out one sheet of filo pastry. With a pastry brush, gently brush the filo pastry with egg and lay another sheet on top. Cut the doubled sheet in half to achieve two even-sized pieces. Brush the top, narrower, edge with egg wash to a depth of about 4 cm. At the other end, spoon 1 dessertspoonful of the curried mixture, leaving a gap of 4–5 cm from the end. Take the left-hand corner of the filo and fold it over the mince, towards the right-hand corner. Fold the semi-covered mince over from right to left and continue thus, working up the strip. Finish with the egg-washed end, which should stick the whole thing together. Repeat this process for the other samosas, but only take out one sheet of filo at a time, and prepare them in batches of two. If you take out all the pastry, it will dry, crack and break.

3. Pour the corn oil into a large pan or deep-fat fryer. If using a saucepan, make sure it is no more than a third full. Heat the oil to a temperature of 180–190°C/350–375°F. When it is at the correct temperature, test it by placing a samosa into the oil. It should bubble but not colour too quickly. They take about 3 minutes to cook. Cook them two at a time and keep warm in the oven. Serve immediately.

Roast Loin of Venison with Red Wine

I love venison; it's a fantastic meat with very little fat. I get mine from a butcher in Totnes who uses a supplier from Exmoor, and it is beautiful. Use the loin from a fallow or roe deer, and ask your butcher to cut off all the sinew and to give you some chopped up bones and trimmings so that you can make the sauce. In the restaurant, I top the venison with a few deep-fried celery leaves for added effect. Glazed Carrots (see page 142) and brussels sprouts are good with this dish; if you really want to show off, however, make some Potato Biscuits too (see page 133).

Serves 4

600-g loin of venison, trimmed

500 g venison bones and trimmings, chopped small

4 tablespoons sunflower oil

1 onion, chopped

2 tablespoons red wine vinegar

1 tablespoon redcurrant jelly

500 ml red wine

500 ml Chicken Stock (see pages 213–14)

1 sprig thyme

½ bay leaf

6 juniper berries, crushed

1 garlic clove, peeled and crushed

salt and freshly milled black pepper

20 g dark (70% cocoa solids) chocolate, grated

Beetroot Garnish

300 g raw beetroot

250 ml water

250 ml cider vinegar

40 g caster sugar

1. Place a large saucepan on the stove to heat. Add 2 tablespoons of sunflower oil and, as soon as it starts to smoke, add the venison bones and trimmings and brown them, stirring from time to time to make sure that they don't burn. Add the onion and cook it until it browns. Tip off any excess fat or oil into a bowl, keeping the bones in the pan. Add the red wine vinegar and stir in the redcurrant jelly. Bring to the boil and reduce the liquid to a sticky syrup that will coat the bones. Be careful not to burn the sugar in the redcurrant jelly. Pour in the red wine and bring back to the boil. Cook for about 3 minutes, then add the chicken stock. Bring back up to the boil and add the thyme, bay leaf, juniper berries and garlic. With a ladle, skim off all the surfacing sediment and discard. Lower the heat to a moderate simmer and cook for an hour, by which time all the flavour will have been extracted from the bones. Pour the liquid through a fine mesh strainer or sieve into another pan. Boil and reduce the liquid by two thirds. You will need about 200 ml of the finished sauce.

2. Peel and grate half the beetroot. Put it in a small pan with the water, vinegar and sugar. Bring to the boil, then lower the heat and simmer for about 10 minutes or until tender. Push the beetroot through a fine sieve into another saucepan, pressing it down firmly to extract all the liquid and flavour.

Discard what's left in the sieve. Bring the beetroot stock to the boil and reduce it to a syrup. Meanwhile, cook the remaining (unpeeled) beetroot in boiling salted water until tender. Strain it into a colander and peel it whilst it is still warm. Cut it into ½ cm dice and add to the beetroot syrup. Set aside.

3. Pour the reduced red wine sauce through a sieve, lined with a muslin cloth to trap all the sediment, into another saucepan. Put the pan on the stove and simmer gently. Season the sauce with some salt and pepper and stir in the chocolate. Do not boil. As soon as the chocolate has melted, remove the pan from the heat and put to one side.

4. Preheat the oven to 200°C/400°F/Gas 6.

5. Season the venison loin with salt and pepper. Place a roasting pan on the stove to heat. Pour in the remaining sunflower oil and, as soon as it starts to smoke, add the loin and brown all over, then put in the oven for about 7 minutes for rare.

6. Warm the sauce but do not allow it to boil; if you do, the chocolate will split and curdle.

7. Heat the beetroot over a high heat. Boil and reduce the stock until it glazes the beetroot. This will take about 5 minutes.

8. Remove the loin from the oven. Place it on a board to relax for about 5 minutes. Lay out four hot dinner plates. Spoon 2 tablespoons of glazed beetroot in the centre of each plate. Cut the loin into four equal pieces and place them on top of the beetroot. Spoon the sauce around the outside. Serve immediately.

Chapter

5. Vegetables

"Salads make easy and nutritious meals, and with all the new varieties of vegetables around, they don't have to be boring." john

You have only to look at the rolling countryside and lush vegetation here to know that it's prime vegetable-growing country. But, unlike in France – where you can see it all growing spectacularly in acres of fields and flat open countryside – here everything is done on a smaller and more discreet scale, though finding where it all happens is just as rewarding. With all the tall hedgerows in the South Hams, a typical journey to a vegetable farm means driving through a network of tiny spider-web lanes surrounded by banks of scented wild flowers, with the open fields hidden from view. You twist and turn until you're dizzy with it all, and then, buried deep in the countryside, you find a tiny cottage industry where the produce is stunning: tender asparagus, young sweet courgettes and plump juicy tomatoes to die for.

I found similar cottage industries during the year I spent in France, working on *French Leave*, and was particularly

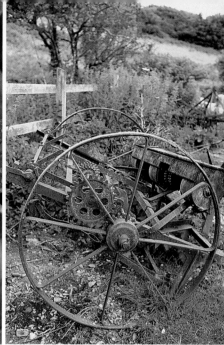

Recent years have seen the introduction of vegetable growing co-operatives in many of England's counties, and Devon is no exception. One of our main suppliers at The New Angel is just such an organisation – made up of thirteen small family-run organic vegetable-growing companies, each of which specialises in different vegetables, including courgettes! Amazing!

impressed by the way many smallholders had pooled their resources to work as co-operatives. I've been delighted to find that this is happening here too. It's places like these, and local farmers' markets everywhere, that have led to such a distinct improvement in the quality of our national veg, and I for one am thrilled about it.

I have always believed that vegetables should be treated with respect. At The New Angel, I prefer to serve them as garnishes that have been carefully chosen for their quality, seasonal freshness and suitability for the main courses they are accompanying. So, when you come here, if you expect to be served a standard dish of veg with your meal, you are likely to be disappointed.

Needless to say, disappointment at not having vegetables is not something I come across much at home, since – with the possible exception of sweetcorn – Kim and I can hardly get the kids to eat them. Charles will eat a piece of cucumber, if pushed, and Kim and Eve do like salads. Vegetables in this country have never been better or more varied. I came across one supplier that produced more than thirty different types of lettuce. And I've just discovered wild ceps and girolles mushrooms growing on Dartmoor and Exmoor. Perhaps we're not that far from France, after all?

Pea and Ham Soup

This is one way to use up surplus ham stock from the cooking of a ham hock (see Ham Hock with Broad Beans in a Parsley Sauce, page 119).

Serves 8 as a starter

1.25 kg fresh peas (or 700 g frozen peas
   if fresh are unavailable), shelled

50 g unsalted butter

1 large onion, finely chopped

100 g ham trimmings

450 ml ham stock

1 pinch sugar

salt and freshly milled black pepper

150 ml double cream

2 tablespoons olive oil

4 slices white bread, crusts removed
   and cut into ½-cm cubes

1. Melt the butter in a saucepan and add the onion. Cook gently for about 5 minutes or until tender. Add the peas and stir. Add the ham trimmings, then cover everything with the ham stock. Bring to the boil and, with a ladle, skim off any surfacing sediment and discard. Lower the heat to a gentle simmer, add the sugar and a little salt and pepper, and cook for a further 10 minutes.

2. Remove the saucepan from the heat and transfer the soup to a liquidiser. Blitz until smooth. Pour the soup into a clean pan, put over a low heat and add the cream.

3. Heat a frying pan on the stove. Add the olive oil and then the bread cubes, and fry until golden. Remove the croutons from the pan with a slotted spoon and dry on kitchen paper.

4. Ladle the soup into eight small soup bowls. Serve the croutons separately.

Peas with Onion and Lettuce

Yet another way of using surplus ham stock from the cooking of a ham hock (see Ham Hock with Broad Beans in a Parsley Sauce, page 119). It is particularly good served with any lamb dish.

Serves 6

70 g unsalted butter

250 g small silver-skinned or pickling onions, peeled

500 g shelled peas (or frozen if fresh are unavailable)

125 ml ham stock

1 teaspoon sugar

salt and freshly milled black pepper

2 lettuce hearts (Little Gems)

1 tablespoon plain flour

2 sprigs parsley, finely chopped

1. Melt 50g of the butter in a large saucepan and add the onions. Cook over a moderate heat for 2 minutes, then add the peas. Pour in the stock and bring to the boil. With a ladle, skim off all the surfacing sediment and discard. Season with the sugar and some salt and coarsely ground black pepper. Reduce the heat to a moderate simmer and cook for a further 10 minutes.

2. Trim the lettuce hearts and lay them on their sides. With a sharp knife, shred them as finely as possible, cutting horizontally across the hearts. Set aside.

3. Soften the remaining butter and put in a bowl. Add the flour and mix until smooth. Gradually add this, a little at a time, to the peas to thicken the sauce, stirring continuously until it is all incorporated and there are no lumps! Add the parsley and the lettuce. Check the seasoning, then transfer to a large bowl and serve immediately.

Cucumber, Mint and Yoghurt Salad

This is an excellent accompaniment to a smoked fish dish such as Pickled Mackerel (see pages 44–5), or cold meats, in which case substitute cheese for the mint. If you chop the cucumber into very fine dice it is also great as a dip for Samosas (see pages 120–1).

Serves 4

1 cucumber
20 g salt
1 sprig mint
150 ml natural yoghurt
salt and freshly milled black pepper
lemon juice

1. To bring out the natural flavour of the cucumber the first thing you need to do is to marinate it in salt. Peel the cucumber, cut it in two, lengthways, then scrape out the seeds with a teaspoon and discard. Rub the salt over the two halves, then leave them on a tray for about 20 minutes. During this time the salt will work like a poultice and pull out all the bitter impurities.

2. Wash the cucumber under cold running water, then dry thoroughly with kitchen paper. Cut it into fine slices and put them in a bowl. Pick the leaves of mint from the stalk, then roll them together. With a very sharp knife, shred them, then sprinkle them onto the cucumber. Stir in the yoghurt, season with a little salt and pepper and add a few drops of lemon juice to taste.

Roast Potatoes

My favourite potatoes for roasting are King Edward. For added flavour, I cook them in goose fat, but if this is not available use lard or a vegetable oil.

Serves 8

2.5 kg potatoes

salt

300 g goose fat

1. Preheat the oven to 200°C/400°F/Gas 6.

2. Peel the potatoes and cut them in half, allowing three halves per person – unless you are cooking for Martha Daisy, who always eats five! Put the potatoes in a large saucepan and cover with water. Add a teaspoon of salt, then put the pan on the stove to boil. As soon as the potatoes are boiling, strain them into a colander and allow them to drain thoroughly.

3. Heat a large roasting tray on the stove and add the goose fat. You will need the fat to be at least 5 mm deep. As the fat begins to smoke, add the potatoes. Using a fork, turn the potatoes over and over in the oil to seal.

4. Put the potatoes in the oven. They will take about an hour to cook and go brown and crisp. After 30 minutes, open the oven and turn the potatoes over in the oil. When cooked, remove from the oven and place in a serving dish using a slotted spoon. Season with salt and serve immediately.

Potato Biscuits

These biscuits are a little bit fiddly but are well worth the trouble. They can be used for garnishing most game dishes, including Roast Loin of Venison with Red Wine (see pages 122–3); they are also good with pheasant, partridge, grouse or hare. Try chives instead of the parsley if you are making them for a game bird dish.

Serves 4

2 large baking potatoes (300g total weight)

25 g unsalted butter

4 egg whites

salt and freshly milled black pepper

1 tablespoon chopped parsley or chives

1. To make the template, use a piece of cardboard – like you did when you watched Blue Peter as a child – and cut out a 5-cm square frame. This will act as the mould when spreading the mixture onto the baking sheet.

2. Bake the potatoes for 40 minutes, or until they are tender, in an oven preheated to 200°C/400°F/Gas 6. Remove the potatoes from the oven and lower the temperature to 180°C/350°F/Gas 4.

3. Peel the potatoes and mash them to a fine purée in a large bowl. Add the butter, stir in the egg whites and season with salt and pepper. Add the parsley or chives and stir to a smooth paste.

4. Line two baking sheets with baking parchment and, using the template, spoon one dessertspoon of the potato mixture into the centre of the square. With a small palette knife, smooth out a thin layer of the mixture covering the whole template. Lift the cardboard and repeat the process. You should be able to get eight potato squares on each baking sheet.

5. Bake the potato biscuits in the oven for about 10 minutes until golden brown. Remove from the oven and allow to cool. Using a palette knife, carefully lift them off the paper. These biscuits will keep for three to four days in an airtight container.

Potato Cake

Choose medium-sized potatoes for this dish, and preferably ones that are all the same size. Serve with Leg of Lamb in a Salt Crust (see pages 112–13) or Roast Pheasant and Ceps Mushrooms (see pages 88–9).

Serves 8

2 kg waxy potatoes (Cara or King
    Edward), peeled
200 ml Clarified Butter
    (see pages 218–19)
salt and freshly milled white pepper

1. Preheat the oven to 220°C/425°F/Gas 7.

2. Grease a 26-cm round cake tin or copper Anna mould with a little clarified butter and put it in the refrigerator to set. Repeat this process to get a good layer of butter on the tin or mould. Remove from the refrigerator.

3. Cut two of the potatoes into slices about 4 mm thick and dry them in a cloth. (You can do this by hand with a knife or with a mandolin cutter, if you have one.) Lay one slice in the middle of the base of the tin, then cover the rest of the base with the remaining slices, making sure they overlap.

4. Cut the remaining potatoes into slices 2 mm thick. Dry them thoroughly in a cloth and place them in a bowl. Pour three quarters of the remaining clarified butter onto the potatoes and toss until they are covered. Season. Pick the largest slices of potato and line the sides of the tin with them, overlapping each slice by about one fifth. Carefully lay the other potatoes in the tin – you should aim for at least six layers – and finish the top layer by arranging the potatoes in a spiral, starting at the centre. Press the potatoes down a little. Brush the remaining clarified butter over the top and cover with a circle of greaseproof paper, cut to fit.

5. Heat a cast iron pan on the stove. When it is white hot, put the tin on top of the pan and place in the oven to bake for about 1 hour. When cooked, the cake should be golden brown in colour. To test if it is cooked, push a small knife into the centre; it should come out easily. Remove the potato cake from the oven and leave it to rest for about 5 minutes. Take off the greaseproof paper and discard. Pour off any excess butter. Run a knife around the edge to loosen it, then place a serving plate on top, turn it over and remove the tin.

Sauté Potatoes

Use waxy potatoes for this dish – a Dutch or Cyprus variety is best. If you don't have any duck fat, use groundnut oil. With the addition of fried onions, this makes a delicious accompaniment to pan-fried liver dishes or grilled kidneys.

Serves 6

1 kg potatoes, washed and scrubbed
75 ml duck fat
50 g unsalted butter
salt
1 teaspoon chopped parsley

1. Put the potatoes into a saucepan and boil for 15–20 minutes, depending on their size. Check they are cooked by sticking a fork into one; if it falls off they are ready. Slightly undercooked is best for this dish. Strain the potatoes into a colander and, when cool enough to handle, peel the skins and cut into 5-mm slices.

2. Heat a large frying pan on the stove. Add the duck fat and, as soon as it starts to smoke, carefully add the potatoes. Cook until the potatoes are coloured a golden brown, shaking the pan from time to time to ensure that they don't stick. This takes about 5 minutes. With a palette knife, carefully turn them over and cook the other side.

3. Pour off any excess fat from the pan and discard, then add the butter. As soon as the butter has melted, toss the potatoes in it. Season with salt and finely sprinkle them with a little chopped parsley. Serve immediately.

Fondant Potatoes

You can use Maris Piper, King Edwards or Cara potatoes for this dish. Serve them with any roast joint as an alternative to roast potatoes.

Serves 8

16 medium-sized potatoes
2 tablespoons groundnut oil
salt and freshly milled black pepper
200 ml Chicken Stock
    (see pages 213–14)
1 sprig fresh thyme
½ bay leaf
1 garlic clove, peeled and crushed
70 g unsalted butter, cut into dice

1. Preheat the oven to 200°C/400°F/Gas 6.

2. Cut off the top and bottom of a potato, hold it with one hand – forefinger at the top and your thumb on the bottom – and, with a small sharp knife, peel it from top to bottom. Remove the peel with one cut of the knife to create a barrel shape, with either five or seven sides, depending on their size. Repeat this process for the other potatoes and put them straight into a bowl of cold water.

3. Place a metal or thick flameproof ceramic casserole dish on the stove to heat. Strain the potatoes into a colander and dry them thoroughly with kitchen paper. Add the oil to the casserole dish and, as soon as it starts to smoke, carefully add the potatoes. Fry the potatoes, moving them around the dish as you do so, for about 5 minutes until they have taken on a little colour. Season with salt and pepper. Pour in the chicken stock and bring to the boil. Add the thyme, bay leaf and garlic clove.

4. Dot the butter over the dish, turn the potatoes over again, then place them in the oven to cook for about 40 minutes (exactly how long will depend on their size). During cooking, the chicken stock will evaporate and glaze the potatoes, so it is very important to move and turn them every 10 minutes or so. You are looking for an even, golden brown colour with the potatoes glazed in chicken juices.

Tomato, Basil and Mozzarella Tart

This makes a great vegetarian dish. Serve as a light lunchtime plate on a hot summer's day, accompanied by a cold glass of Chablis.

Serves 4

300 g or 1 sheet puff pastry
  (see page 213)
8 plum tomatoes
2 shallots, finely chopped
1 garlic clove, peeled and chopped
a little olive oil
salt and freshly milled black pepper
1 teaspoon sugar
4 basil leaves
4 teaspoons tapenade
2 x 125-g Mozzarella cheeses
40 g rocket leaves
1 teaspoon Tarragon Vinaigrette
  (see page 219)
40 g Parmesan cheese

1. Preheat the oven to 220°C/425°F/Gas 7.

2. Lightly dust a work surface with flour and roll out the pastry. Cut into four rounds about 12 cm in diameter, prick all over with a fork, then place on a baking sheet. Cover with baking parchment and then another baking sheet. Bake in the oven for about 8 minutes until golden brown. Remove and put to one side.

3. Cut four of the tomatoes into quarters, remove the seeds and roughly dice the flesh.

4. Heat a little olive oil in a pan on the stove and soften the shallots and garlic but do not allow them to colour. Add the tomato flesh and cook gently for about 10 minutes until a thick purée is obtained. Season with salt, pepper and the teaspoon of sugar. Remove the pan from the heat. Shred half of the basil and add to the purée.

5. Spread the tapenade over the pastry discs and cover with the tomato purée. Slice the remaining tomatoes and arrange them on top of the purée. Season with salt and black pepper. Shred the remaining basil and sprinkle some over each tart. Place in the oven for 5 minutes to warm through.

6. In the meantime drain the Mozzarella and slice thinly. Turn the grill on full. Remove the tarts from the oven and carefully lay the Mozzarella slices on top.

7. Place the tarts under the grill to melt the cheese but do not brown. When the cheese is hot and bubbling remove from the grill and immediately transfer to warm plates. Top with rocket leaves in the vinaigrette, and Parmesan curls, and serve.

Tomato Consommé

I call this a tomato consommé because it is completely clear. It isn't really a consommé, however, as no clarification is involved. It is particularly good as a pretty starter for a summer's meal, either lunch or dinner. For the best colour and flavour, it is always best to use tomatoes that have seen the most sun. They should be soft and deep red. To add texture, you can add little balls of cooked carrot, courgette and potato. Or float some cooked, cold vermicelli or similar pasta. I like to serve it in glass bowls that have been thoroughly chilled in the freezer. Alternatively, crush a quantity of ice and fill eight soup plates. Place a smaller bowl on top of the ice and then fill them with the consommé. It can also be served in coffee cups, as an appetiser. Garnished or not it's very refreshing. I like to accompany it with choux buns piped with Boursin or cream cheese.

Serves 8 as a starter

1 litre Chicken Stock (see pages
   213–14), all surface fat removed
2 kg over ripe, soft tomatoes
4 garlic cloves
1 bunch fresh basil
1 teaspoon salt
1 teaspoon caster sugar
freshly milled black pepper
3–4 drops Tabasco
3–4 drops Worcestershire sauce
1 pinch celery salt

Variation

For a completely vegetarian dish, substitute Vegetable Stock (see page 216) for the Chicken Stock.

1. Line a colander with a double layer of muslin cloth, allowing plenty of cloth to overlap the sides so that it can be gathered and picked up when full. Place a large bowl underneath.

2. Place a third of the chicken stock, plus a third of the tomatoes and a third of the seasonings in a liquidiser and blitz to a smooth pulp. Pour the tomato pulp into the muslin cloth, then repeat the process for the other ingredients, transferring the tomato pulp into the muslin cloth each time.

3. Gather the overhanging cloth and tie the ends together with some string, leaving a long piece of string about 50 cm in length. Carefully lift the muslin bag and, using the piece of string, tie it to a handle on a kitchen cupboard, or some other suitable handle, and position the bowl underneath. The weight of the pulp will cause the consommé to drip through the muslin into the bowl. Let the consommé filter through for at least 2 hours.

4. Discard the bag of pulp – there will be no flavour or nutrients left – and put the clear, pink consommé in the fridge to chill for at least an hour.

Onion Tart

This dish makes a great main course served with a salad.

Serves 6

350 g shortcrust pastry (see page 213)

30 g bacon, cut into ½-cm lardons

60 ml olive oil

2 large onions or 6 shallots, finely
sliced

1 garlic clove, peeled and finely
chopped

1 sprig fresh thyme

¼ bay leaf

60 ml dry white wine

90 g White Sauce (see page 216)

2 sprigs parsley, finely chopped

1 egg yolk

salt and freshly milled black pepper

90 g Emmenthal or Gruyère cheese,
grated

1. Preheat the oven to 180°C/350°F/Gas 4.

2. Roll out the pastry and line an 18 x 4 cm deep tart tin. Line it with foil, fill with baking beans and blind bake in the oven for 15 minutes or until the pastry is dry. Remove the tin from the oven and put it on a rack to cool.

3. Put a small saucepan of water on the stove to boil. When boiling, add the bacon lardons. Bring the pan back to the boil and immediately strain through a sieve over the sink. Put to one side to cool.

4. Place a frying pan on the stove, add the olive oil and, as soon as it starts to smoke, add the onion and garlic and fry them until golden brown; this takes about 10 minutes. Add the lardons, the thyme and the ¼ bay leaf. Pour in the wine and boil it until it has been reduced to a syrup. Stir in the white sauce and continue to cook until it has been completely absorbed into the mixture. Remove the pan from the stove and stir in the parsley, followed by the egg yolk – this will give the mixture richness and help to glaze the tart. Season with a little salt and pepper.

5. Carefully remove the foil and baking beans from the tart base. Pour in the onion mixture and sprinkle the top with the grated cheese. Turn on the grill and, when it is hot, glaze the tart until it is crisp. Serve immediately.

Glazed Carrots

A delicious way to make ordinary carrots more exciting!

Serves 8

750 g large carrots
1 sprig fresh tarragon
50 g unsalted butter
1 teaspoon sugar
salt and freshly milled black pepper
100 ml water
1 teaspoon chopped flat-leaf parsley

1. Top and tail the carrots, and peel them. Cut into pieces 5 cm long x 6 mm thick and put in a large saucepan. Add the sprig of tarragon and butter, and season with the sugar and some salt and pepper.

2. Pour in the water; it should come about a third of the way up the carrots. Put the pan on the stove over a high heat and bring to the boil. Allow all the water to boil off, tossing the carrots from time to time. This takes about 10 minutes.

3. At this point the carrots will start to fry in the butter and sugar; toss them again. When they are glazed, and cooked but still retain a little bite, sprinkle them with the chopped parsley. Serve.

Jerusalem Artichoke Mash

Preserve the vitamin C content of artichokes by adding them to boiling water.

400 g small Jerusalem artichokes, peeled
125 g unsalted butter, cut into dice
100 ml double cream
salt and freshly milled black pepper

1. Bring a pan of salted water to the boil. Add the artichokes, boil for 5 minutes, then immediately strain. Pour the hot blanched artichokes into another saucepan. Add the butter and the cream and put the pan on the stove to boil. Stir occasionally to prevent the artichokes sticking to the bottom. Simmer for 20 minutes until tender. The cream will thicken and reduce by half.

2. Pour the artichokes into a blender and blitz until smooth. Season, then scrape back into the saucepan using a spatula. Cover with a butter paper or greaseproof paper until ready to serve.

Jerusalem Artichoke Soup

I love the slightly earthy flavour of the Jerusalem artichoke. It is such an underrated and versatile vegetable. Jerusalem artichokes contain as much vitamin C as new potatoes and can be used in as many different ways as potatoes – for fish, meat, game, poultry and vegetarian dishes. Serve the soup straight away with some crunchy bread. I like to add a few drops of truffle oil to each bowl. Dried, ground cep mushrooms sprinkled on the top are also delicious. Alternatively, watercress or parsley sauce spooned into the soup at the last minute looks good and adds another dimension. You can also froth the soup by using a hand-held blender at the last minute to give a different 'cappuccino' appearance and texture.

Serves 8

1 kg Jerusalem artichokes
juice of 1 lemon
100 g unsalted butter
salt and freshly milled black pepper
1 onion, chopped
2 garlic cloves, peeled and crushed
½ bay leaf
1 sprig thyme
1 sprig fresh tarragon
500 ml milk
800 ml Chicken Stock
    (see pages 213–14)
250 ml double cream

1. Fill a large bowl with water and add the lemon juice; this will stop the artichokes discolouring. Peel the artichokes with a small knife or vegetable peeler, then slice them, putting them into the lemon water as you do so.

2. Melt the butter in a large lidded saucepan. Drain the artichokes, put them in the pan and season with salt and pepper. Add the onions, along with the garlic, bay leaf, thyme and tarragon. Cover with the lid and cook gently for about 15 minutes. Stir from time to time to prevent the artichokes burning.

3. Bring the milk to the boil in another saucepan, then stir it into the artichokes. Add the chicken stock and bring the soup to the boil. With a ladle, skim off any surfacing sediment and discard. Lower the heat to a moderate simmer and cook for about 20 minutes or until the artichokes are tender.

4. Transfer the soup to a liquidiser and blitz until smooth. Pour it through a fine sieve into another pan and check the seasoning. A little lemon juice helps to bring out the flavour. Bring the soup back up to the boil, stir in the cream, then serve.

Dittisham Asparagus Spears with Poached Egg and Hollandaise

The asparagus season is a very short one; it starts in May and only lasts six weeks. As with all other fresh produce, asparagus is best when it is in season.

Serves 4

800 g fresh asparagus spears

1 dessertspoon malt vinegar

4 eggs

25 g unsalted butter

salt and freshly milled black pepper

1 quantity of Hollandaise Sauce (see pages 217–18), being kept warm in a bowl over a pan of hot water

1 sprig fresh chervil

1. Peel the asparagus from just below the tip to the end of the stalk using a vegetable peeler. Take care not to peel too deeply – keep the stalk intact.

2. Half fill a saucepan with salted water and bring to the boil. When boiling, add the asparagus spears and cook for 4 minutes or until tender but still retaining a bite. Remove the pan from the heat. Strain the asparagus and refresh in cold running water. Strain again and put to one side.

3. Place another pan of water on the stove to boil. Add the malt vinegar and a large pinch of salt. When the water is boiling, place a dessertspoon in the centre of the water and stir with a circular action to create a whirlpool effect. Crack the eggs into the water; the whirlpool current will in turn move the egg whites and the eggs will form a neat circular shape. Lower the heat to a moderate simmer and poach the eggs for about 3 minutes.

4. Place a frying pan on the stove to heat and add the butter. As soon as it starts to melt, add the asparagus and season with salt and pepper. They will take about 2 minutes to warm through.

5. Lay out four large plates. Place six spears of asparagus in the centre of each. With a slotted spoon, carefully lift out the eggs, cutting away any excess egg white from around the yolk. Place them on top of the asparagus piles. Spoon the hollandaise sauce over the eggs and top each with a little sprig of fresh chervil. Serve immediately.

Wild Mushroom Risotto

The most important thing to remember when making a risotto is to buy the best rice. I have used Aquerello rice in this dish, the beauty of which is that it is organic and has been aged for over a year in sealed vats. The rice is, therefore, far less starchy, creamier, holds its shape well and absorbs more stock. This makes for an excellent risotto.

Serves 6

2 tablespoons olive oil

2 shallots, finely chopped

200 g Aquerello carnaroli rice

20 g dried morel or cep mushrooms

100 ml dry white wine

600 ml Chicken Stock
   (see pages 213–14)

100 g mascarpone cheese

20 g unsalted butter

40 g fresh wild mushrooms

salt and freshly milled black pepper

70 g Parmigiano Reggiano

20 g rocket leaves

3 teaspoons truffle oil

1. Heat the olive oil in a pan on the stove, add the shallots and allow them to soften but not colour. Stir in the rice and cook gently for 2 minutes to allow the rice grains to absorb the oil. Add the dried mushrooms (these help to accentuate the flavour), pour in the wine and, over a medium heat, stir occasionally until the wine has evaporated.

2. Gradually add the stock – about 150 ml at a time – allowing the rice to absorb the stock slowly before adding any more. The rice will swell and become creamy, plump and tender. Stir occasionally but not too often. When the rice is tender, stir in the mascarpone cheese.

3. In a separate pan, add the butter and sauté the mushrooms over a high heat for about 2 minutes until golden. Season with salt and pepper, then add to the rice. Check the seasoning, and adjust if necessary.

4. To serve, place a 7-cm wide by 3-cm deep ring in the centre of each plate or bowl and fill with the hot rice, pressing down well. Grate over the Parmigiano or, with a swivel peeler, make curls and place on top of the rice.

5. Assemble a handful of rocket leaves drizzled with truffle oil on top of the rice and cheese. Carefully remove the ring and serve with a little more truffle oil spooned around the outer edge of the risotto.

Piccalilli

I have included this recipe because I love piccalilli. Make a large amount and store it in sterilised Kilner jars; it will keep for up to three months. It's great with Cheddar cheese, cooked ham, pork pies, ham hock and countless other dishes. The vegetables first need to be soaked overnight in pickling brine.

Makes 2 litres

Pickling Vinegar

600 ml white wine vinegar

15 g red chillies, diced

250 g caster sugar

50 g grated horseradish

1 sprig fresh thyme

1 bay leaf

Vegetables

300 g red peppers

200 g yellow peppers

200 g cucumber

200 g courgettes

200 g button onions

200 g fennel

200 g celery

2 litres cold water

300 g salt

10 g chillies, finely diced

18 g cornflour

15 g turmeric

75 g Dijon mustard

1. To make the pickling vinegar, pour the white wine vinegar into saucepan. Add all the remaining ingredients and bring them to the boil. As soon as the vinegar has boiled, remove the pan from the heat and leave it to cool. During this time the aromatics and herbs will infuse and flavour the vinegar. When cold, strain the vinegar through a muslin cloth and refrigerate until required.

2. Trim, wash and cut all the vegetables into large 1.5-cm cubes. Place them in a large plastic container with the 2 litres of water and the salt. This is the pickling brine. Leave them to soak overnight.

3. Drain the vegetables and wash them thoroughly. Drain again.

4. Pour the pickling vinegar into a large saucepan and bring to the boil. Put the chillies in a small bowl and add the cornflour and turmeric. Add a small amount of the boiled vinegar and whisk it to a smooth paste (there should be no lumps). With a spatula, add this thickening and colouring mixture to the vinegar and whisk vigorously until smooth. Remove the pan from the heat. Stir in the mustard and add the vegetables.

5. With a ladle, fill the jars, leaving the lids open until the piccalilli is cold. Cut a small circle of greaseproof paper to fit on the top of the piccalilli, then close and seal the lids. Store in the refrigerator for at least a week to allow the piccalilli to infuse and absorb all the flavours.

Chapter
6. Pudding

Puddings have always held pride of place in British cuisine. Treacle tart, fruit pies and bread and butter pudding are pretty much national institutions – and rightly so. There is something about our winning combinations of fruit and high-quality dairy produce that's unbeatable. What more perfect dessert is there, after all, than that English pairing of fresh seasonal strawberries served with lashings of cream?

When it comes to fruit and dairy produce, Devon is a shining example of the best that England has to offer. Lush sweet grass and the finest dairy cows make for sumptuous cream and butter, while the iron-rich soil, combined with traditional organic farming methods and mild winters, has resulted in sublime fruits. Blackberries grow wild in the hedgerows, and blackcurrants, strawberries, blueberries and raspberries (Kim's favourite) are all produced organically on small-scale allotments. Tree fruits, such as damsons, pears,

Creamy dairy produce – the country's finest – is a key ingredient in many of my favourite puddings. And so are eggs – I'm very lucky in this respect because there's a chap called Paul Vincent from Dittisham who keeps Warren hens and brings me the best eggs I have ever tasted. Fresh custard made from these local ingredients is absolutely delicious – it's no wonder that Charles is addicted!

apples, plums and quinces all thrive happily, too. Local success stories include the famous South Devon red plum, the Dittisham Ploughman – the key ingredient in the delicious local plum liqueurs – and many different varieties of apple from the wonderful orchards at Capton.

The great thing about this section of the book is that it's got something for everyone. As far as I'm concerned, whatever our quibbles over fish, seafood and vegetables, desserts are definitely something we eat as a family. Most people, after all, love their puds. My kids certainly do – Amelia, in particular, loves lemon tart – but they also, thankfully, like fruit. In fact, they're real gannets for it. We have huge fruit bowls all over the place that are constantly raided. It's a habit I always encourage, although it doesn't always work with Charles, who definitely veers towards the unhealthier options. Charles can drink custard by the bowlful (we're talking real custard here, thickened with egg yolks) and he has a love of chocolate that borders on the obsessive. He has a little cupboard behind his bed where he hoards the stuff, often for months. We all still talk about the night he put a chocolate egg under his pillow then lay down on it and went to sleep. The chocolate melted all over the sheets and Kim was not best pleased!

Chocolate Soufflés

If you want something extra special, you could serve these with a hot chocolate sauce or white chocolate ice cream, though they are delicious just as they are.

Serves 6

40 g unsalted butter

30 g dark (70% cocoa solids) chocolate, finely grated

80 g Pastry Cream (see page 220)

20 g cocoa powder

2 egg yolks

5 egg whites

75 g caster sugar

icing sugar, to dust

1. Melt the butter and, using a small pastry brush, brush the insides of six soufflé moulds or ramekins, 4 cm deep by 8 cm across. Sprinkle the finely grated chocolate over the butter to coat the insides, tapping out any excess. Place in the refrigerator to set.

2. Preheat the oven to 180°C/350°F/Gas 4.

3. Put the pastry cream in a large bowl and whisk until smooth. Whisk in the cocoa powder. Add the egg yolks and whisk them into the mixture until smooth.

4. Put the egg whites into a mixing bowl and whisk them until they start to firm and turn white in colour. Sprinkle in the caster sugar, a little at a time, until a smooth meringue is achieved. Do not over whisk the egg whites or they will become granular and the soufflés will not rise properly. Very gently fold the egg whites into the chocolate mixture.

5. Remove the soufflé moulds from the refrigerator and fill them to the top, leaving the edges clean or the soufflés will catch as they are rising and cook unevenly – use your index finger and thumb to wipe around the top edge of the moulds. Put the soufflés on a baking sheet and cook them in the hot oven for 7 minutes. They should double their size and feel firm to the touch. Remove from the oven and dust with icing sugar. Serve immediately.

Charles's Chocolate Mousse

The kids will love it!

Serves 8

280 g dark (70% cocoa solids) chocolate

60 g unsalted butter, cut into small dice

8 egg whites

60 g caster sugar

4 egg yolks

280 ml double cream

1. Chop 240 g of the chocolate and place it in a heatproof (Pyrex) bowl. Add the butter and place the bowl over a saucepan half filled with water. Gently melt the chocolate and butter, stirring the mixture until it's smooth. Do this as slowly as possible; if the chocolate is allowed to get too hot it becomes granular.

2. Whisk the egg whites until they turn white with soft peaks, then add the sugar. Again, do not over

whisk the whites or you will end up with a very granular mousse.

3. Stir the egg yolks into the chocolate, a third at a time. Fold in the egg whites until they are fully incorporated into the melted chocolate. Using a spatula, pour the chocolate mousse into a large glass bowl and put in the refrigerator for an hour to set. (It will keep for up to two days if covered with cling film.)

4. When ready to serve, whip the cream until firm and spoon it over the chocolate mousse. Grate the remaining chocolate over the cream. Or let your children have fun with the decorating!

Coffee Caramels

Crème caramel is one of the most famous classic desserts. Adding coffee to it gives another dimension. Try it – you'll be hooked.

Serves 6

Caramel
120 g caster sugar
90 ml water

Custard
500 ml milk
60 g caster sugar
4 eggs (small)
10 g instant coffee granules

1. First make the caramel. Put the sugar and half the water in a small saucepan and place it on the stove to boil. When the sugar starts to colour (it will become dark golden), quickly remove the pan from the heat and add the remaining water. This will stop the sugar from becoming darker. Put the pan back on the heat. Remove it as soon as it starts to boil again. Pour a little of the caramel into the bottom of six lightly buttered 8-cm ramekin dishes and allow to set.

2. Preheat the oven to 120°C/250°F/Gas ½.

3. Pour the milk into a saucepan and warm. Put the sugar and eggs in a bowl and whisk them until smooth. Stir the coffee granules into the warm milk and then pour the coffee-flavoured milk into the eggs, stirring all the time. With a ladle, remove all the surfacing foam and discard. Pour the mixture into the ramekins, cover them with cling film, and put in a deep roasting tray. Carefully pour boiling water into the tray to within 1 cm of the top of the ramekins, then place in the oven for about 35 minutes until the custard has set. Remove the ramekins from the baking tray, allow them to cool, then refrigerate for at least 4 hours before serving.

4. To serve, remove the cling film from the ramekins. Gently press down around the edges of the custards and shake them free. Turn them upside down into the centre of a small bowl, allowing all of the caramel to pour out over the top of the desserts.

Fried Bread and Butter Pudding

You can serve bread and butter pudding hot, with vanilla sauce or even ice-cream.

Serves 8

30 ml Calvados

1 x 400-g brioche loaf, crusts removed
and cut into 1½-cm thick slices

50 g unsalted butter

4 eggs

100 g caster sugar

½ vanilla pod

300 ml double cream

300 ml milk

30 g sultanas, soaked overnight in
Calvados

Apple Sauce

2 Bramley apples, peeled, cored and
cut into small pieces

70 g caster sugar

200 ml water

½ vanilla pod

Vanilla Sauce

250 ml single cream

1 vanilla pod

3 egg yolks

50 g caster sugar

To Serve

demerara sugar

20 g unsalted butter

1. Preheat the oven to 120°C/250°F/Gas ½. Lightly butter a 10 x 25-cm terrine or pâté mould and line it with greaseproof paper.

2. Spread the brioche slices with the butter, then cut each slice into four.

3. Crack the eggs into a bowl and beat in the caster sugar. Cut a vanilla pod in two, lengthways, and scrape out the seeds from one half. Add them to the eggs and sugar. Pour the cream and the milk into a saucepan. Add the scraped vanilla pod and warm over a gentle heat. Pour over the eggs and whisk until they have been fully incorporated into the liquid. Strain the custard through a fine mesh sieve into a jug. With a ladle, skim off all the surface foam and discard.

4. Place a layer of buttered brioche in the base of the terrine mould. Sprinkle a few sultanas over the brioche and then pour enough custard over the brioche to soak it through. Repeat this process until all the brioche, sultanas and custard have been used. Cover the terrine mould with butter papers or foil, allow it to stand for 5 minutes, then put it onto a baking sheet and place in the oven for about 45 minutes. When the pudding is cooked, leave it to cool, then refrigerate. It will keep for at least two or three days.

5. Put the apples in a stainless steel lidded saucepan. Add the water, sugar and ½ a vanilla pod (split into two, lengthways). Cover with the lid and cook over a gentle heat until the apples have become a pulp. Pour into a bowl and whisk until it is completely smooth. Remove the vanilla pod. Allow to cool, then refrigerate until needed.

6. Next make the vanilla sauce. Pour the cream into a saucepan. Cut the vanilla pod into two, scrape out all the seeds, and add them, plus the pods, to the cream. Put the cream on the stove to boil. Meanwhile, whisk together the egg yolks and sugar until pale in colour. When the cream has boiled, remove it from the heat and pour a little over the eggs, mixing it together well. Pour this back into the saucepan with the cream and place the pan back onto the stove over a gentle heat. With a wooden spoon, stir the custard continuously until it has thickened enough to coat the back of the spoon. You must not, at any stage, let the sauce boil. This will take about 10 minutes. Remove the custard from the heat and pour it through a fine mesh sieve into a bowl. Allow to cool, then cover with cling film and refrigerate until needed.

7. To serve, turn out the cold bread and butter pudding onto a wooden chopping board. Take off the greaseproof paper and cut into slices about 2 cm thick. Dip each slice into demerara sugar. Preheat the oven to 190°C/375°F/Gas 5.

8. Melt the butter in a heavy cast iron frying pan. As the butter starts to froth, add a slice of pudding and cook it on both sides until the sugar caramelises. Transfer the slice to a baking sheet. Repeat the process for the other slices and then put the tray in the oven to bake for about 5 minutes.

9. Lay out eight dessert plates. Cover half the plate with apple sauce and the other half with vanilla sauce. Remove the slices of pudding from the oven and carefully place a slice in the centre of each plate. Wow!

Steamed Syrup Sponge

My mother used to make this pudding for me when I was young (a long time ago!) and I loved it. You can use either beef suet or butter for this dish; I prefer butter. Serve with lashings of hot Custard (see page 220).

Serves 4

40 ml golden syrup
175 g self-raising flour
75 g cold butter or beef suet
50 g caster sugar
zest of 1 lemon
1 pinch salt
1 egg
100 ml milk

1. Grease a 1-litre pudding basin with a little softened butter. Pour the golden syrup into the bottom of the basin.

2. Sieve the flour into a mixing bowl, then add the butter or suet, the caster sugar, lemon zest and salt. Rub the ingredients together until you have a mixture that looks like breadcrumbs.

3. Crack the egg into another bowl, beat it until smooth, then stir in the milk. Pour this gradually into the flour and beat together thoroughly for

about ten minutes; the mixture should look like
soft butter. Pour it into the pudding basin. Cover
the top with greaseproof paper and a sheet of
foil and secure with string.

4. Place a trivet or an upturned saucer in the
base of a large lidded saucepan – it is important
to keep the pudding off the bottom or it will
burn. Put the basin on top and carefully pour in
enough boiling water to come two-thirds of the
way up the sides. Cover with the lid and steam
over a moderate heat for about 1½ hours. It will
be necessary to add a little more boiling water
to the pan from time to time. Always try and
keep the water at a constant level.

5. Take the saucepan off the heat and carefully
lift the basin out of the water. Cut the string and
remove the foil and greaseproof paper. Place a
plate over the top of the basin and turn the
pudding upside down onto a serving plate.

My Banoffee Pie

When making this dish, don't cut the bananas too soon – they will discolour quickly. If the jelly has set before you use it, just warm it a little before coating the banana.

Serves 6

Biscuit Base
125 g Butter Biscuits (see page 201)
30 g demerara sugar
30 g raisins
30 g unsalted butter, melted

Fromage Frais
2 leaves of gelatine
1 egg yolk
30 ml water
40 g caster sugar
200 g fromage frais
100 ml whipping cream

Passion Fruit Jelly
1 leaf of gelatine
2 passion fruit
juice of 1 orange
20 ml water
30 g caster sugar

3 bananas

1. First make the biscuit base. Finely crush the biscuits using a rolling pin and place the crumbs in a bowl. Mix in the demerara sugar and raisins, then stir in the melted butter. Put an 18 x 5 cm ring mould onto a cake board. Spoon the biscuit mixture into the ring and press it down as firmly as possible using the back of a spoon. Put in the refrigerator for about 30 minutes to set.

2. Next make the fromage frais. Soak the gelatine in cold water to soften. Put the egg yolk into a bowl. Pour the water and sugar into a small saucepan and bring to the boil on the stove. As soon as it has boiled, remove the pan from the heat. Slowly pour two-thirds of the syrup over the egg yolk, whisking rapidly all the time. Continue whisking the yolk until it has become pale in colour and thick in texture. Set aside.

3. Add the softened gelantine leaves to the remaining syrup and warm on the stove to dissolve. Set aside to cool slightly. In another bowl, whisk the fromage frais until smooth.

4. Pour the melted gelatine into the egg mixture, whisking all the time. In yet another bowl whisk the cream until it has just peaked. Using a spatula, fold the cream into the egg, then fold in the fromage frais until it is completely mixed and smooth. Pour the fromage frais over the biscuit base. Level the top with a palette knife and place in the refrigerator for at least 4 hours to set.

5. Meanwhile, make the passion fruit jelly. Soak the gelatine in cold water to soften. Cut the passion fruit in half and, with a teaspoon, remove the fleshy seeds and put them in a bowl. Discard the shells. Squeeze the orange juice into a pan and add the water and sugar. Put the pan on the stove and bring to a simmer. With a ladle, remove all the surfacing impurities and discard, then take the pan off the heat. Add the softened gelatine leaf, stirring to dissolve, then pour this juice over the passion fruit and mix together. Set aside to cool and begin to set.

6. Cut the bananas into 3-mm slices. Remove the biscuit base from the refrigerator. Arrange the sliced bananas over the top of the surface of the fromage frais. Ladle the passion fruit jelly over the bananas and put back in the refrigerator for at least an hour to set. To serve, carefully remove the ring mould by running a warm knife around the inside edge of the ring. Cut the tart into six and serve immediately.

Baked Apricot Upside Down Pudding

This is best served with Custard (see page 220).

Serves 6

Sponge
150 g unsalted butter, cut into small
    pieces
150 g caster sugar
zest of 1 orange
3 eggs
225 g plain flour
12 g baking powder
6 apricots, halved and stoned

Apricot Sauce
6 apricots, halved and stoned
100 g caster sugar
juice of 1 orange

1. Preheat the oven to 220°C/425°F/Gas 7 and lightly grease a 20-cm pie dish with some softened butter.

2. Put the diced butter into a mixing bowl, add the caster sugar and beat together until pale in colour and creamy in texture. Add the orange zest, then beat in the eggs, one at a time, until smooth. Sift the flour and the baking powder into the mixture and, using a spatula, mix until smooth.

3. Lay the apricots, cut side down, in the base of the pie dish. Pour the sponge mixture over the top and bake in the oven for about 50 minutes.

4. Meanwhile, prepare the sauce. Put the apricots into a saucepan. Add the sugar and, using a fine sieve, squeeze the juice from the orange over the apricots. Put the pan on the stove, bring to the boil and cook, stirring all the time, for about 5 minutes. Lower the heat and allow the apricots to gently cook for a further 10 minutes.

5. Pour the stewed apricots into a liquidiser and blitz them until they form a smooth purée. Pour the purée into a fine mesh sieve set over a bowl and push it through the sieve. This will trap any skin that was not liquidised. Pour the sauce into a sauce boat.

6. Remove the apricot sponge from the oven and leave it to stand for about 5 minutes. Run a palette knife around the edge of the sponge. Place a large plate on top and very quickly turn the sponge upside down. Carefully remove the pie dish. Cut the sponge into six equal pieces and lay them in the centre of each plate. Serve a little hot custard on one side and a little apricot sauce on the other.

Devon Clotted Cream Ice Cream

If you have children, a little table-top ice cream machine is essential. Home-made ice cream is full of good ingredients – milk, cream and eggs. Charles will not eat an egg boiled, scrambled or fried, but he will eat gallons of home-made ice cream! Do not throw away the vanilla pod – it can be used to make vanilla sugar. Just place the pod into a jar, cover with caster sugar and seal. After a week the sugar will take the flavour and smell of the vanilla. Great in cakes, sweet sauces and jams.

Makes about 1.5 litres

600 ml full-fat milk

600 ml Devon clotted cream

60 ml liquid glucose

1 vanilla pod

240 g egg yolks (approximately 8 eggs)

240 g caster sugar

Variations

The possibilities are endless.

• If you want a less rich ice cream use semi-skimmed milk and substitute ordinary double cream for the Devon clotted cream.

• To make a delicious chocolate ice cream, dispense with the vanilla pod and add 1 tablespoon of cocoa and 150 g of melted dark (70% cocoa solids) chocolate to the boiled milk.

• For a rich caramel ice cream, add caramelised sugar instead of plain caster sugar.

1. Put the milk, cream and glucose in a saucepan. Cut the vanilla pod in two, lengthways, and, with the point of a sharp knife, scrape out the seeds and add to the milk. Put the pan on the stove to boil and, as soon as it reaches boiling point, take it off the heat.

2. Place the egg yolks in a bowl, add the sugar and whisk together until pale in colour and thick in texture. This takes about 7 minutes using a food mixer – twice as long by hand! Whisk the milk and cream into the egg yolks and sugar, then pour the mixture back into the saucepan.

3. Stir the mixture continuously over a low heat until it is thick enough to coat the back of a spoon. You must not allow the mixture to boil or the eggs will scramble and it will be ruined. Strain the mixture through a fine sieve into a clean bowl and allow to cool.

4. When cold, pour the mixture into your ice cream machine and churn it. It will take about 40 minutes to ice and thicken. Spoon into a plastic container and place in the the freezer. It will be ready to eat after 1 or 2 hours.

Apple and Blackberry Pie

This pie is lovely served with a puddle of double cream.

Serves 6

½ quantity of Sweet Pastry
(see page 213)

Filling
450 g peeled and cored Bramley
apples, cut into quarters
100 g caster sugar
100 g blackberries

1. Preheat the oven to 230°C/450°F/Gas 8.

2. Place the apples in a bowl, then add the caster sugar and blackberries. Gently toss them together, making sure that the apples are completely covered in sugar.

3. Lightly butter a 25-cm round pie dish. Remove the pastry from the refrigerator. Cut a 200-g piece for the base of the pie, leaving 300 g for the top. Lightly dust a worktop with flour, then roll out each piece of pastry to a rough circle, to a thickness of about 3 mm.

4. Lay the smaller circle of pastry in the base of the pie dish and gently press it down. Spoon the apple and blackberry filling into the centre of the pastry, leaving a 2-cm border around the edge. With a pastry brush, brush a little water around the border and upper edge of the pastry. Carefully place the larger pastry circle over the filling and gently press down around the edge to seal the border. Cut off any excess pastry with a palette knife. Using your forefinger and thumb, crimp the edges of the pastry to ensure a good seal.

5. Lightly brush the top of the pie with water and sprinkle with a level dessertspoon of caster sugar. With the point of a knife, make a small cut in the centre of the pie for the steam to escape. Cook in the oven for 45 minutes or until golden.

Toffee Apples

You have to make these for your children for Bonfire Night!

Makes 6

6 small dessert apples (Coxes)
6 wooden sticks
225 g demerara sugar
1 tablespoon golden syrup
30 g unsalted butter
2 teaspoons lemon juice
2 tablespoons water

1. Wash the apples and dry thoroughly with kitchen paper. Remove the stalks and push a wooden stick into the centre of each.

2. Line a baking sheet with oiled greaseproof or baking parchment.

3. Put half the sugar, syrup, butter, lemon juice and water into a heavy-based saucepan and put on the stove to heat, stirring all the time. Bring to the boil and boil rapidly until the temperature reaches 130°C/275°F. Remove the pan from the heat and place on a heatproof surface or stand. One at a time, quickly dip the apples into the toffee until evenly coated, lift out and let the excess toffee drip back into the pan.

4. Stand the apples on the lined baking sheet and leave to set in a cool dry place. The toffee will become soft and sticky if left in a hot and steamy kitchen.

Crown of Strawberries

This is a great dessert to have in late spring or early summer. A large version also makes a great birthday cake – just follow the recipe, but use a 16-cm ring mould instead of 6-cm cutters, and, of course, pipe a birthday message on top!

Serves 8

500-g Swiss Roll Sponge cut into
   8 x 6 cm discs (see page 189)
30 g strawberry jam
250 g Shortbread biscuits
   (see page 194)
20 g icing sugar
40 small strawberries

Mousse Filling
150 g fromage blanc
120 ml whipping cream
70 ml Stock Syrup (see page 220)
1 egg yolk
1½ leaves of gelatine, soaked in cold
   water to soften

Strawberry Sauce
110 g very ripe strawberries
60 g icing sugar
20 g shelled pistachio nuts
75 g white almond paste or marzipan

1. Using a 6-cm plain cutter, cut out eight rounds of sponge; they should be the same size as the shortbread biscuits. With a small palette knife, spread a layer of jam over the top of the sponge discs and place them, jam side down, onto the shortbread. Place eight 6-cm ring moulds on a tray. Put the sponge and shortbread 'sandwiches' in the base of each mould, making sure the shortbread is on the bottom.

2. Sift the icing sugar into a bowl. Keep back eight of the best strawberries for garnishing. Wash and hull the remaining 32. Slice them in half, lengthways, place them in the bowl and roll them in the icing sugar.

3. Line each mould with the halved strawberries, pressing them gently, flat side down, against the inside rim, leaving the centre free for the cream filling. Keep any strawberries and juice that are left over for the sauce.

4. Next make the mousse filling. Whisk the fromage blanc in a bowl until smooth. Pour the cream into another bowl and whisk until it forms stiff peaks. Put both to one side.

5. Put the stock syrup in a saucepan and bring to the boil. Put the egg yolk in a bowl and whisk with the boiled syrup until the mixture turns a pale, almost white, colour and becomes thick.

6. Pour 20 ml of water into a small saucepan and warm it on the stove. Add the soaked gelatine and stir until the gelatine has completely dissolved. Fold this liquid, a little at a time, into the fromage blanc. Then fold in the egg mixture and, finally, the whipped cream. Spoon the mousse into the moulds, level the tops with a palette knife, and place in the refrigerator for at least 4 hours to set.

7. Next make the strawberry sauce. Wash and hull the 110 g of strawberries. Place them in a liquidiser, adding any strawberries left over earlier, and blitz them to a smooth sauce. This should take about 2 minutes. Strain through a fine sieve, then refrigerate until needed.

8. Put another small pan of water on the stove to boil. When boiling, add the pistachio nuts and scald them in the boiling water for 2 minutes. Remove the pan from the heat, strain the pistachios through a sieve, then cool them under cold running water. Place the nuts in a clean, dry cloth and rub them together to remove their skins. Cut into fine dice and mix into the almond paste. Lightly dust a work surface with a little icing sugar and roll out the paste as thinly as possible, to a thickness of

about 1 mm. Again using a plain cutter, cut out eight 6-cm circles. Lightly dust a tray with icing sugar and, using a palette knife, place the discs on it. Leave them, uncovered, for about 1 hour, to dry a little.

9. Lay out eight plates. Remove the mousses from the refrigerator. Spoon a little strawberry sauce into the centre of each plate and place a mousse (still in its mould) on top. Remove the ring moulds by rubbing the outside with a cloth dipped in hot water and carefully lifting them off. Top each mousse with a pistachio and marzipan 'lid'. Roll the remaining eight strawberries in a little extra icing sugar, then cut them in half, lengthways, with the green stalk attached. Place two halves on top of each dessert. Serve immediately.

Cold Strawberry Rice Pudding

This is Olivia's favourite pudding. She no longer buys tinned creamed rice!

Serves 8

Rice
60 g short grain rice
20 g unsalted butter
600 ml milk
1 vanilla pod, split lengthways
1 leaf of gelatine
100 ml double cream
30 g caster sugar

Strawberry Sauce
500 g strawberries, hulled
50 g icing sugar

Strawberry Jelly
1½ leaves of gelatine
50 g caster sugar
80 ml water
125 ml strawberry purée

30 strawberries, hulled and cut in two, lengthways
sprigs mint, to garnish

1. Wash the rice in cold water and strain through a sieve. Put it into a saucepan, add the butter and heat until the butter has melted. Pour in the milk, then add the vanilla pod. Bring the milk to the boil, stirring occasionally, then lower the heat to a simmer and gently cook the rice for 25 minutes.

2. Soak the gelatine leaf in cold water to soften.

3. Pour the cream into the rice and continue simmering for a further 5 minutes. Add the softened gelatine and the caster sugar. Stir the rice until the gelatine has fully dissolved. Take the pan off the heat and remove the vanilla pod.

4. Line a shallow roasting tray with greaseproof paper and lay out eight 7.5 x 3.5 cm ring moulds. Fill the moulds with the rice pudding and place in the refrigerator to set for about 1 hour.

5. Make the strawberry sauce. Blitz the strawberries to a smooth pulp in a liquidiser. Pass the pulp through a fine mesh strainer (to trap the seeds) into a glass bowl. Reserve 125 ml of the pulp for the strawberry jelly. Add the icing sugar to the remaining pulp and stir until dissolved. Taste the sauce. It may need a little more sugar, depending on the ripeness of the fruit. Refrigerate.

6. Next make the strawberry jelly. Place the gelatine leaves in cold water to soften. Put the caster sugar and water in a small pan and bring to the boil. As soon as it boils, remove the pan from the heat and stir in the softened gelatine leaves. Add the reserved strawberry pulp, then strain through a muslin cloth into a clean bowl.

7. Remove the rice pudding from the refrigerator and top each one with five strawberry halves, cut side down. Spoon the strawberry jelly over the strawberries and refrigerate for a further 2 hours.

8. To serve, lay out eight dessert plates. Take the cold strawberry rice puddings out of the refrigerator and, using a fish slice, place in the centre of each plate. Spoon the strawberry sauce around the moulds. Dip a small, sharp knife into boiling water and very carefully cut around the top edge of each mould. Gently pull up the ring mould. Slice each of the remaining strawberries very thinly into six, lengthways, and lay around the outer edge of each moulded rice pudding. Top each dessert with a little sprig of mint.

Strawberry and Pink Rhubarb Soup

I use the pink, or forced, variety of rhubarb in this dish, which is grown in the dark so that it produces narrow, light pink shoots. It is usually available around Easter time, so buy some, cut away the leaves, trim the bottom of the stalk, wash and cut into 4-cm pieces, then bag it up and freeze until the strawberry season starts in late May.

Serves 4

400 g washed and cut rhubarb
80 g caster sugar
juice of 1 lime
32 strawberries
100 g caster sugar
4 sprigs mint

1. Place the rhubarb in a large lidded saucepan. Add the sugar, then squeeze and strain the lime juice over the top. Cover with the lid and shake the rhubarb to coat it in sugar. Place the pan on the stove and cook on a fairly high heat for about 15 minutes. Stir occasionally so that it does not catch on the bottom. When the rhubarb is soft, remove it from the heat and spoon it into a liquidiser. Blitz until smooth, then pour into a bowl to cool. Cover with cling film and refrigerate.

2. Put four soup bowls in the freezer to chill for about 1 hour. Wash the strawberries and roll them in the caster sugar. Remove the bowls from the freezer and pile up eight strawberries on top of each other in the centre of the bowls. With a ladle, carefully pour the rhubarb soup around the strawberries and top each one with a sprig of mint.

Raspberry Meringues

Like strawberries, raspberries should only be bought when in season in Britain. I have tasted some relatively good Spanish and French fruit, but the strawberries from South America, which are available in supermarkets all the year round, are, I think, acidic and tasteless.

Serves 6

Meringues

110 g egg whites (approximately 4 eggs)
110 g caster sugar, plus extra for dusting
110 g icing sugar

Filling and sauce

300 g fresh raspberries
250 ml double cream
25 g caster sugar
50 g hazelnuts, toasted and crushed
    (optional)
sprigs of mints, to garnish

1. Preheat the oven to 110°C/225°F/Gas ¼. Line a baking sheet with greaseproof paper or baking parchment.

2. Thoroughly clean a mixing bowl – it is best to use lemon juice and kitchen paper to eliminate any grease. Check the egg whites for any evidence of yolk, then pour them into the bowl and whisk briskly until you have soft peaks, then slowly add the caster sugar, whisking continuously until stiff. Sift in the icing sugar and, with a slotted spoon, carefully fold in to the egg whites, taking care not to over mix.

3. Fill a piping bag fitted with a star nozzle with the meringue mixture and pipe 12 round meringues, about 7 cm in diameter, onto the lined baking sheet. Alternatively, use a large spoon. Bake in the oven for 60 minutes. Remove and allow to cool.

4. Put half of the raspberries and half of the remaining sugar in a liquidiser and blitz until you have a purée. Strain through a fine sieve into a bowl to remove the pips, then set aside.

5. Pour the double cream into a bowl and whisk with the remaining sugar until thick but not stiff. Spoon the whipped cream onto six of the meringues, then sandwich them together with the remaining six. Place on large plates. Sprinkle with the remaining raspberries and drizzle over the raspberry sauce. Finish by sprinkling over some crushed toasted hazelnuts and top each one with a sprig of mint and a dusting of icing sugar.

Kim's Raspberry Mousse

Kim's favourite red fruit are raspberries. You can use strawberries in just the same way, if you prefer!

Serves 6

4 leaves of gelatine
3 eggs
60 g caster sugar
250 ml milk
500 g raspberries
250 g double cream
icing sugar to taste
6 sprigs mint

1. Soak the gelatine in cold water to soften.

2. Separate the eggs, put the yolks in a mixing bowl and keep the egg whites in a small bowl in the refrigerator for later. Add the caster sugar to the egg yolks and whisk them until light in colour.

3. Pour the milk into a saucepan and bring to the boil. When boiling, remove the milk from the heat and pour it over the egg yolks and sugar. Whisk them together, then pour this custard back into the saucepan. Return the pan to the stove over a low heat and cook, stirring with a wooden spoon, until it thickens and coats the back of the spoon. It must not boil or the custard will scramble and be ruined. This process takes 5 minutes. Remove the custard from the heat and pour it through a fine mesh sieve into a bowl.

4. Remove the gelatine from the water and squeeze off any excess. Stir it into the custard until it has fully dissolved. Leave to cool then refrigerate for 1 hour to set.

5. Carefully wash the raspberries, reserving 18 of the best ones for decoration. Put the remaining raspberries in a liquidiser and blitz them until smooth. Pour the raspberry pulp through a fine mesh sieve and into a clean glass bowl. This will trap the seeds. Measure 250 g of the raspberry pulp, keeping the remaining for later.

6. When the custard is almost set, fold in the 250 g of raspberry pulp until smooth. Pour the cream into a mixing bowl and whisk to a soft piping consistency. Fold this into the raspberry custard. Pour the egg whites into a mixing bowl, whisk to soft peaks, then carefully fold into the raspberry mousse. Pour the mousse into six large wine glasses and put them in the refrigerator to set for 2 hours.

7. Add about 2 dessertspoons of icing sugar to the remaining raspberry pulp (the amount you need will depend on how sweet you want it to taste). Add the garnishing raspberries to this pulp and turn them over to coat. Spoon three raspberries and a spoon or two of the pulp over the finished mousses just prior to serving. Top them with a small sprig of fresh mint.

Black Cherry Custard Tart

This is best served accompanied by a large spoonful of whipped cream.

Serves 6–8

300 g Sweet Pastry (see page 213)

500 g fresh black cherries, stoned

20 g ground almonds

2 whole eggs

1 egg yolk

100 g caster sugar

100 ml milk

125 ml double cream

25 ml Kirsch

250 ml whipped cream, to serve

1. On a lightly floured surface, roll out the sweet pastry to a thickness of 5 mm, then line a lightly greased 19 x 3 cm deep tart ring. Trim off any excess pastry from the edge and place on a tray lined with greaseproof paper. Allow to rest in the refrigerator for 20 minutes.

2. Preheat the oven 220°C/425°F/Gas 7.

3. Remove the pastry case from the refrigerator, place a large sheet of greaseproof paper in the base and half fill it with baking beans. Put in the oven and cook for 12 minutes, then remove and leave to cool slightly. Carefully remove the beans and greaseproof paper and put the pastry case back in the oven to continue baking for a further 6 minutes or until it is dry. Remove and set aside to cool. Lower the oven temperature to 200°C/400°F/Gas 6.

4. Place the cherries into the base of the pastry case and sprinkle them with the ground almonds. Crack the eggs into a bowl and add the egg yolk, then add the sugar and whisk together. Pour the milk and cream into a saucepan and put on the stove to boil. As soon as it reaches boiling point, remove from the heat and pour over the eggs, stirring until smooth. Add the Kirsch. Pour the custard through a strainer into a jug and, with a small ladle, skim off the surfacing foam. Carefully pour the custard into the tart over the cherries, filling it to the top, then bake in the oven for about 20 minutes until the custard is set. Remove the tart from the oven and leave it to cool in the ring mould.

5. When cold, dust with icing sugar, then place under a hot grill to glaze. This should take about 2 minutes. Carefully remove tart ring and keep the tart in the refrigerator until needed.

Pink Grapefruit Ice

This makes either a refreshing dessert after a heavy winter meal or a light dessert for a summer's lunch.

Serves 4

8 pink grapefruit
125 ml water
170 g caster sugar
1 large sprig mint

Variation

You can substitute 8 oranges for the pink grapefruit (it's the same number because oranges yield more juice).

1. Cut off the skin from two of the grapefruits using the following method. Cut a 5-mm slice off the top and bottom. With a very sharp knife, cut top to bottom, following the contours of the fruit. With your knife behind the white pith, cut again until all the skin and pith has been removed. You will see a membrane between each segment of fruit. Over a bowl, make a cut inside the membrane and another inside the next one and remove the segment. Repeat until you have segmented both grapefruits. Squeeze the remaining flesh over the segments, to extract all the juice, and put to one side.

2. Cut the remaining grapefruits in half and squeeze the juice into a separate bowl.

3. Put the water and sugar in a small saucepan, place on the stove and bring to the boil. When boiling, remove the pan from the heat. Add the syrup to the squeezed grapefruit juice, a ladleful at a time. Taste the juice regularly; it must not be too sharp. Depending on the sweetness of the grapefruits, you may not need to add all the syrup. Strain the grapefruit syrup through a fine sieve into a shallow plastic container and place in the freezer for 2 hours.

4. Remove the grapefruit ice from the freezer and, with a whisk, break up the mixture into even ice crystals. Return it to the freezer. Repeat this process another two times.

5. To serve, put four small plates in the freezer to chill. When chilled, place a 120-mm plain cutter in the centre of each plate. Spoon the grapefruit ice into the cutters and press down. Arrange the grapefruit segments on top of the ice. Pick the leaves from the mint stalks and shred finely. Carefully remove the cutters and sprinkle the tops of the grapefruit with the mint. Serve immediately.

Lemon Tart

This makes a light, refreshing dessert any time of the year. I like to make my tart slightly sharp, but if you prefer something sweeter, just add more sugar. To achieve the best result, make the filling the night before, so that the lemon has time to infuse the cream and give the tart more depth of flavour. A long time ago I used to use shortcake biscuit to make the base, but in that case it has to be eaten the same day. In this recipe I have used a basic sweet pastry instead. I like to serve it in the restaurant with a ball of lemon sorbet and some candied lemon zest. Devon clotted cream also goes extremely well with it.

Serves 8

500 g Sweet Pastry (see page 213)
1 tablespoon icing sugar, to dust

Lemon Cream
9 large eggs
200 g caster sugar
zest of 2 lemons
juice of 4 lemons
300 ml whipping cream

Variation

If you prefer, you can make this tart with limes, but remember that limes have a stronger flavour, so reduce the quantity by half. Pink grapefruit also work well – use the juice of two.

1. Roll out the pastry and use it to line a 28-cm tart tin. Cover the base with a circle of greaseproof paper and fill with baking beans or rice. Allow to relax in the refrigerator for at least an hour before blind baking in an oven preheated to 180°C/350°F/Gas 4 for 25 minutes or until the pastry is golden and dry to the touch. Set aside.

2. Crack the eggs into a bowl and whisk until smooth. Add the sugar and whisk again. Add the grated zest of two lemons, being careful not to grate in the white pith underneath the skin or the filling will taste bitter and ruin the tart. Cut the lemons in half and squeeze them through a fine sieve into the egg mixture. Discard all the trapped lemon pips. Whisk in the whipping cream, then, with a small ladle, skim off all the surfacing foam and discard. For best results, put the finished lemon cream in the refrigerator to infuse, ideally overnight.

3. Preheat the oven to 140°C/275°F/Gas 1.

4. Pour the mixture into the tart ring and bake it in the oven for about 25 minutes. After this time, check the tart. It should feel wobbly and only part set. Remove from the oven and place it on a board. As it cools it will set.

5. When cold, dust with the icing sugar then, using a blowtorch, flame the sugar to caramelise. This will give the tart a crisp top, adding a delicious contrast to the texture of the filling.

Coconut Creams

Like the Coffee Caramels (see page 156) this is a variation on the classic crème caramel recipe. The coconut complements the red fruits and adds a delicious, slightly oriental flavour.

Serves 4

250 ml coconut milk (Thai)

250 ml milk

4 eggs (small)

60 g caster sugar

40 g desiccated coconut

150 g raspberries

150 g strawberries

12 cherries, with stalks

50 g redcurrants

90 g icing sugar

1. Preheat the oven to 190°C/375°F/Gas 5.

2. Pour the coconut milk and the milk into a saucepan and put on the stove to warm. Crack the eggs into a mixing bowl, add the sugar and whisk together until smooth. Gently stir in the warm milk. Skim off all of the surface foam with a ladle and discard. Pour the coconut custard into four 8-cm ramekins, cover with cling film and put into a deep roasting tray. Carefully pour boiling water into the tray to within 1 cm of the top of the ramekins. Place on the bottom shelf of the oven and bake for 50 minutes or until set. Carefully remove the ramekins from the water and allow to cool, then refrigerate for at least 1 hour.

3. Increase the oven temperature to 260°C/500°F/Gas 9.

4. Sprinkle the desiccated coconut onto a baking tray and place in the oven. After about 4 minutes the coconut will turn a light golden colour. Remove the toasted coconut and put it into a bowl for later.

5. Put half the red fruit and all of the cherries (including their stalks) into a bowl. Cover the remaining berries with the icing sugar and blitz in the liquidiser until smooth. Pour the pulp through a fine mesh sieve over the whole fruit, discarding the trapped seeds. Refrigerate.

6. Lay out four dessert plates. Remove the creams from the refrigerator and take off the cling film. Gently press down around the edges of the moulds, shake them free and then turn them upside down onto the centre of each plate. Sprinkle with the toasted coconut. Spoon the cold red fruits around the edge of the creams and serve immediately.

Chapter
7. Home Bakes

" Breadmaking may seem time-consuming, but I find kneading can be incredibly therapeutic, especially after a busy day.**"** john

In many ways, this chapter is one of the most personal in the book, containing as it does an odd mixture of staples, family favourites and some great British classics. It is also partly a celebration of our national institution: tea-time. Doughnuts, Eccles cakes and biscuits are all here, plus, of course, the most exquisite tea of them all, the cream tea. No chapter about home-baking in Devon could possibly be complete without a recipe for that made-in-heaven combination of fabulous scones, chunky home-made strawberry jam and rich yellow clotted cream.

There are some personal bugbears here, too, one of which is Bakewell Tart, which, although not native to Devon, is often, in my opinion, cooked incorrectly, with too much sponge and royal icing, so I've included here what I consider to be an improved version. The other, more important bugbear, is bread. Ever since I came back from France I've

In these days of shop-bought bread and ready-made cakes (many of them excellent), home-baking can seem like a bit of a hassle. But there's nothing to equal the smell and taste of freshly baked bread, biscuits and cakes cooking in the oven. I love it – and I guarantee that any kind of baking at home will make you popular with your family!

been looking for a good British loaf with no starch, E numbers or other additives, and they're pretty thin on the ground. At The New Angel, we've managed to source traditional stoneground flour, which we blend with pain de campagne flour with fantastic results. Bread happens to be one of my particular passions, so I've included several recipes here – one for soda, one for brown, one for white and one for my personal favourite, sourdough – do try it!

Home-baking is a big hit at home, where Olivia and Martha, in particular, adore eating the results. They've got a running battle going over doughnuts at the moment. Olivia can eat one in seven seconds flat, and Martha holds the all-time record of eating eleven in one sitting. On a more serious note, I find it a great way of introducing children to cooking. It's not only fun, it also gives the children a tremendous sense of achievement when they manage to make small individual items such as pasties and scones. We've had several successful – though not, it must be admitted, entirely chaos-free – baking sessions, where Eliza, Charles and Amelia have emerged from the kitchen covered in flour and looking very pleased with themselves. And when it comes to making cake mixtures, there's no one who doesn't like licking the spoon!

Martha Daisy's Doughnuts

I remember as a child the smells of the doughnut machines at the fairground – with queues of children all around. These are Martha's favourites.

Makes 12

225 g strong white flour

1 pinch salt

40 g unsalted butter

120 ml milk

1 egg

15 g caster sugar

15 g fresh yeast

120 g raspberry or strawberry jam

200 g caster sugar, for coating the doughnuts

1. Sieve the flour and salt into a large mixing bowl.

2. Melt the butter in a saucepan over a gentle heat. Remove the pan from the stove. Pour in the milk, whisk in the egg, and add the sugar.

3. Crumble the yeast into the flour, pour in the milk and butter mixture, then beat the resulting dough in a food mixer for about 10 minutes until smooth. Place the dough in a clean bowl and cover with a damp clean cloth. Place somewhere warm (such as an airing cupboard) to prove for about 1 hour, by which time the dough should have doubled in size and feel light and spongy to the touch.

4. Turn out onto a lightly floured surface. Gently knead the dough by hand to form a smooth ball, then, with a rolling pin, roll it out to a thickness of 1½ cm. Cut the dough into 12 equal pieces, weighing approximately 35 g each. Roll each doughnut until it is smooth and perfectly round. Put onto a lightly floured baking sheet and place somewhere warm to prove for a further 25 minutes.

5. Place a large, deep pan one-third full of vegetable oil on the stove to heat. When hot (170–180°C/ 325–350°F), place four of the doughnuts at a time into the oil. Make sure the oil is not too hot or the doughnuts will colour too quickly. Turn them with a metal slotted spoon. They will take about 8 minutes to cook. Remove from the oil and drain on kitchen paper. When cold, insert the point of a small knife into the side of each one, to a depth of 3 cm. Fill a piping bag, fitted with a small plain nozzle, with the jam and pipe 10 g of jam into each doughnut.

6. Roll each doughnut in caster sugar until the outsides are completely covered. Eat fresh.

Chocolate Brownies

The kids love these at the weekends and they only take a little time to prepare. They are always best made the day before and covered with chocolate on the day you are going to eat them. If you cut them small, they make a great treat with a cup of coffee at the end of a dinner party – something different instead of serving chocolates.

Serves all of them for the weekend!

350 g unsalted butter, cut into
    small pieces
350 g brown sugar
4 eggs
100 g cocoa powder
100 g self-raising flour
100 g walnuts

Chocolate Topping
200 ml double cream
250 g dark (70% cocoa solids)
    chocolate
50 g unsalted butter

1. Preheat the oven to 180°C/350°F/Gas 4.

2. Put the butter in a mixing bowl, then add the sugar and beat together until soft in texture and pale in colour.

3. Crack the eggs into another bowl and whisk until smooth, then add to the butter and sugar mixture. Then, whisking continuously, add the cocoa powder. Carefully fold in the flour and stir in the walnuts.

4. Line two shallow trays with baking parchment, pour in the mixture and bake for about 25 minutes, or until crisp on top but still soft in the middle. Remove from the oven and turn them out onto a rack to cool. When cold, wrap in cling film and store in a dry place.

5. For the chocolate topping, pour the cream into a saucepan and heat. Remove from the stove as soon as it comes to the boil. Break up the chocolate with a rolling pin and add it to the boiled cream. Stir until fully dissolved and smooth. Add the butter and, again, keep stirring until it has dissolved. Allow to cool.

6. To finish, remove the cling film from the brownies and put them back in the baking trays. Pour half the chocolate over one tray and, with a palette knife, coat the top evenly. Repeat for the other tray. Put the chocolate brownies in the refrigerator for about an hour to set, then cut to any size you want.

Swiss Roll Sponge

I mainly use this as a base to mousses, as in the case of the Crown of Strawberries (see page 170–1), but you can also use it to give added texture to other desserts, and to soak up syrups or alcohol to give another flavour. You can, of course, roll it with a cream filling to make a delicious Swiss roll. It will keep for up to three days in the refrigerator and can also be frozen.

Makes 500 g

150 g icing sugar
150 g ground almonds
3 whole eggs
3 egg yolks
9 egg whites
115 g caster sugar
120 g plain flour

1. Preheat the oven to 200°C/400°F/Gas 6. Line two baking sheets with greaseproof paper or baking parchment.

2. Sift the icing sugar into a bowl and add the ground almonds. Crack the whole eggs into another bowl and add the three egg yolks. Whisk them together, gradually adding the icing sugar and ground almonds as you do so, and beat until pale in colour and thick in texture.

3. In a separate bowl, whisk the egg whites and caster sugar to soft peaks. Gently fold into the egg and almond mixture. Carefully fold in the flour. Divide the mixture equally between the two baking sheets, spread it level with a palette knife, then bake in the oven for 14 minutes until golden.

4. Remove from the oven and turn upside down onto a wire rack to cool. Peel off the paper and, when cold, wrap in cling film and use as required.

Scones with Home-made Strawberry Jam and Fresh Vanilla Cream

A great big pot of strong English Breakfast Tea and hungry people are the only requirements for this dish!

Serves 6

Jam
300 g strawberries, hulled
300 g caster sugar

Vanilla Cream
300 ml Devon clotted cream
30 g caster sugar
seeds of ½ vanilla pod

Scones
300 g plain flour
25 g baking powder
100 g unsalted butter, cut into dice
50 g sultanas
200 ml milk
1 egg
100 g vanilla sugar

1. Put the strawberries in a saucepan with the caster sugar and crush them with a fork. Put the pan on the stove and bring to the boil. Remove the scum that comes to the surface with a spoon. Reduce the jam until it becomes quite thick, then pour it into a bowl and allow to cool. Refrigerate until needed.

2. Whisk the cream with the sugar and vanilla until it thickens, then transfer it to a serving bowl, cover with cling film and refrigerate.

3. Preheat the oven to 200°C/400°F/Gas 6. Sieve the flour and baking powder together into a large bowl. Add the butter and rub it into the flour until the mixture resembles breadcrumbs. Add the sultanas. Pour the milk into a saucepan and warm it gently over a low heat. Remove the pan from the stove. Whisk in the egg and sugar and pour the liquid into the flour, mixing it all together. Leave the dough to stand for 5 minutes, then turn it out onto a lightly floured work surface and knead it together to form a smooth ball. Roll out the dough into a rectangle with a thickness of about 1.5 cm. With a 6-cm plain cutter, cut out 12 scones and place them upside down onto a floured baking sheet. Lightly dust the scones with some more flour, then leave them to stand for a further 10 minutes before cooking. During this time the baking powder will begin to act like yeast does in bread.

4. Cook the scones in the preheated oven until golden brown; they will take about 12 minutes. Serve them just warm with the strawberry jam and lashings of cream.

Eccles Cakes

My grandmother used to make these for me. Being a gruesome child, I used to call them fly cemeteries! I like to eat them warm with a dollop of whipped cream.

Serves 8

200 g Puff Pastry (see page 213)

30 g unsalted butter

80 g caster sugar

grated zest and juice of 1 lemon

½ teaspoon mixed spice

50 g currants

50 g raisins

25 g mixed peel

1 egg white

1. Cut the pastry into eight equal parts. On a lightly floured surface, roll each piece of pastry into a disc approximately 10 cm x 1 mm.

2. Gently melt the butter in a saucepan. Remove from the heat and stir in 50 g of sugar, the lemon juice and zest, the mixed spice, currants, raisins and mixed peel. Spoon the fruit mixture onto the centre of the pastry discs. Lightly brush the edges of the pastry with cold water, then draw the edges together to enclose and seal the fruit. Turn the cakes over and, one by one, press them inside a floured 6-cm plain cutter to give them a uniform shape. Place on a baking sheet, then put into the refrigerator for 10 minutes to rest.

3. Preheat the oven to 220°C/425°F/Gas 7.

4. Remove the baking sheet from the refrigerator. Brush each cake with egg white, sprinkle liberally with the remaining caster sugar and make three 4-cm cuts on the top of each cake. Bake in the oven for about 12 minutes or until golden brown and crisp. Allow to cool slightly before serving.

Bakewell Tart

You can serve this either warm with a good English Custard (see page 220) or cold, straight from the refrigerator.

Serves 6

250 g Sweet Pastry (see page 213)
70 g raspberry jam
100 g unsalted butter, cut into dice
100 g caster sugar
2 eggs
100 g ground almonds
10 g plain flour
10 g flaked almonds
90 g icing sugar
20 ml water

1. Lightly butter an 18.5-cm flan ring. Roll out the pastry on a lightly floured work surface into a 28-cm circle with a thickness of about 3 mm. Lay the pastry over the flan ring and carefully line the inside. Trim off any excess pastry and save it for later. Put the pastry case and trimmings in the refrigerator. After about 10 minutes, remove the pastry case and pour the raspberry jam into the bottom, spreading it carefully over the base, then put it back in the refrigerator.

2. Preheat the oven to 200°C/400°F/Gas 6.

3. Place the butter in a bowl, add the sugar and beat together until creamy and white. Beat in the eggs, one at a time, and then add the ground almonds. Beat until smooth. Add the flour and mix until smooth. Remove the pastry case from the refrigerator and pour in the almond mixture.

4. Roll out the pastry trimming to a thickness of about 2 mm and cut into six strips about 18 cm in length and 1 cm in width. Lay the strips over the tart to make a lattice pattern. Trim away any overlapping pieces. Sprinkle the top with the flaked almonds. Put the tart on a baking sheet, place in the oven and cook for about 35 minutes or until it is well risen and golden brown in colour. Remove from the oven and allow to cool slightly. Mix the icing sugar and water together and brush over the tart.

Shortbread

These biscuits are great with a cup of tea.

Makes 8 (250 g)

120 g plain flour

75 g caster sugar

120 g unsalted butter, cut into 1-cm
  dice, softened

1 egg yolk

1. Place the flour, sugar and butter in a bowl and rub together between your hands until the mixture becomes granular and resembles coarse breadcrumbs. Mix in the egg yolk to bind the pastry together. Wrap in cling film and refrigerate for at least 1 hour to allow it to relax.

2. Preheat the oven to 160°C/325°F/Gas 3. Line a baking tray with greaseproof paper or baking parchment.

3. Lightly dust a work surface with flour, and roll out the pastry to a thickness of about 5 mm. Using a 6-cm plain cutter, cut out eight rounds of shortbread, and place them on the baking tray. Bake in the oven for 15–20 minutes or until they look dry but not coloured.

4. Remove the shortbread from the oven and, whilst hot, sprinkle each biscuit with caster sugar. Shortbread is very fragile when hot, so leave the biscuits to cool before attempting to pick them up.

Grandmother's Cake

This is a recipe that my grandmother passed on to me when I was small. I've been known to eat so much of it that I've felt physically sick – I suppose that's the sort of thing you do when you are a child! I don't know why, but my grandmother always makes it better than me. Store in an airtight container for one to two days before eating, to let the cake mature and moisten.

Serves 6

225 g plain flour
½ teaspoon baking powder
275 g natural glacé cherries, quartered
115 g ground almonds
225 g caster sugar
225 g unsalted butter, softened
4 eggs, at room temperature
grated zest and juice of 1 lemon
12 sugar cubes, coarsely crushed

1. Preheat the oven to 180°C/350°F/Gas 4. Line a 20-cm round cake tin with greaseproof paper or baking parchment.

2. Sift the flour and baking powder into a bowl. In a separate bowl, toss the cherries with the ground almonds. In another mixing bowl, add the sugar and butter and beat together until pale and fluffy. Add the flour and slowly beat in the eggs, one at a time. Stop the food mixer and carefully fold in the cherries and almonds by hand. Sprinkle in a little lemon juice and zest.

3. Spoon the mixture into the cake tin and, using a spatula, level off the top. Sprinkle with the crushed sugar cubes and bake in the oven for 1 hour, then cover with a sheet of brown paper or foil and continue to bake for a further 30 minutes or until the cake has shrunk away from the sides. Leave to cool in the tin for about 15 minutes before turning out on a wire rack to cool completely.

Aunt Sadie's Soda Bread

Kim, being half Irish, loves soda bread. In Ireland, scones, wheaten bread and soda bread are all made with buttermilk. If you have difficulty obtaining this, just add a tablespoon of lemon juice or cider vinegar to 300 ml of full-fat milk. Soda bread is best eaten on the day of baking. Try it in the morning with some home-made strawberry jam (see page 190).

Makes 1 loaf

250 g strong white flour

250 g wholemeal flour

1 teaspoon bicarbonate of soda

1 teaspoon salt

35 g unsalted butter, cut into dice

300 ml buttermilk

1. Sift both flours into a large bowl. Add the bicarbonate of soda and salt. Add the butter and gently rub it into the flour until the mixture resembles breadcrumbs. Make a well in the centre and pour in the buttermilk. Stir the mixture together to form a soft dough. Turn out onto a lightly floured work surface and knead for 3–4 minutes until the dough becomes elastic.

2. Preheat the oven to 200°C/400°F/Gas 6.

3. Roll the dough to form a ball, then push it down to flatten it slightly. Make a 2-cm deep cross on the top, dust with a little flour and bake in the oven for about 35 minutes. When cooked, it should sound hollow when tapped. Place on a wire rack, covered with a cloth, to cool.

Kim's Blueberry Muffins

These are Kim's favourites.

Makes 12

500 g plain flour

1 tablespoon baking powder

2 teaspoons custard powder

225 g caster sugar

185 g fresh blueberries

2 eggs

185 ml milk

185 ml sunflower oil

icing sugar, for dusting

1. Preheat the oven to 190°C/375°F/Gas 5. Grease a muffin tin with butter and dust with flour, shaking out any excess.

2. Sift the flour, baking powder and custard powder into a large bowl. Add the sugar and blueberries. In a separate bowl, mix together the eggs, milk and oil. Make a well in the dry ingredients, add the milk mixture and combine, taking care not to over mix. Spoon the batter into the prepared muffin tins and bake in the oven for 15–20 minutes or until golden. Serve dusted with icing sugar.

Carrot Cake Muffins

Makes 12

435 g plain flour

165 g soft brown sugar

1 teaspoon baking powder

½ teaspoon bicarbonate of soda

½ teaspoon salt

1 teaspoon ground cinnamon

1 pinch mace

125 ml cooking oil

125 ml crushed pineapple

1 egg

1½ teaspoons vanilla essence

500 g grated carrot

125 g raisins

Icing

125 g cream cheese

1 tablespoon butter icing sugar

1 pinch mace

1. Preheat the oven to 200°C/400°F/Gas 6. Grease a muffin tin with butter and dust with flour, shaking out any excess.

2. Sift the flour into a large bowl and mix in the brown sugar, baking powder, bicarbonate of soda, salt, cinnamon and mace. In a separate bowl, mix together the oil, pineapple, egg and vanilla essence. Make a well in the centre of the dry ingredients and add the pineapple mixture. Stir thoroughly to combine. Finally fold in the carrot and raisins. Spoon the batter into the prepared muffin tins and bake in the oven for 15–20 minutes or until golden.

3. Remove the muffins from the oven, place on a wire rack and allow to cool. Cream the icing ingredients together in a bowl, and spoon over the muffins before serving.

Shirley's Ginger Pear Muffins

These are my mum's favourite. Muffins are great for breakfast accompanied by a big cappuccino.

Makes 12

500 g plain flour

125 g soft brown sugar

1 teaspoon bicarbonate of soda

½ teaspoon salt

2 teaspoons ground ginger

1 teaspoon ground cinnamon

1 pinch ground nutmeg

1 pinch ground cloves

250 ml natural yoghurt

125 ml sunflower oil

3 tablespoons treacle or molasses

1 egg, beaten

375 g diced pear

125 g raisins

60 g chopped walnuts

1. Preheat the oven to 200°C/400°F/Gas 6. Grease a muffin tin with butter and dust with flour, shaking out any excess.

2. Sift the flour into a large bowl, add the brown sugar, bicarbonate of soda, salt, ginger, cinnamon, nutmeg and cloves, and mix together. In a separate bowl, mix together the yoghurt, oil, molasses and egg. Make a well in the centre of the dry ingredients and add the yoghurt mixture. Stir to combine, then fold in the pears, raisins and walnuts. Spoon the batter into the prepared muffin tins and bake in the oven for 20 minutes or until risen and golden.

Butter Biscuits

These are a real treat with a good strong cup of tea in the afternoon. Piped small, they are also great as petits fours after dinner.

Makes 6

225 g unsalted butter, cut into dice, softened
110 g icing sugar
350 g plain flour

1. Preheat the oven to 190°C/375°F/Gas 5.

2. Place the butter in a mixing bowl, add the icing sugar and beat until white in colour. This will take about 10 minutes. Sieve the flour, then beat it into the butter and sugar until the mixture is light and fluffy. This will take a further 5 minutes.

3. Lay out six 5 cm x 1.5 cm deep ring moulds on a flat baking tray lined with baking parchment. Fill a piping bag fitted with a large plain nozzle with the mixture. Pipe the mixture into the moulds, then bake in the oven for about 20 minutes. Allow to cool, then remove the ring moulds and, using a palette knife, lift them from the paper onto a serving plate.

Sourdough Bread

Sourdough bread is one of my favourite kinds of bread. I always think it has more flavour than other types. This recipe is divided into two simple stages. Firstly, you will need to make what is called a 'starter'. This starter should be left for at least two days, after which a proportion of it is added to the basic dough, giving it its flavour. Traditionally, this bread was proved in a straw or cane basket lined with a linen cloth sprinkled with flour. It was then baked in a wood-burning brick oven. The linen-lined basket is great – if you can get it – as it ensures a good shape. You simply turn the dough out upside down onto a hot tray or a plate.

Makes 1 loaf

Starter

3 teaspoons dried yeast or 25 g fresh
    yeast
325 ml tepid water
250 g strong white flour

Dough

1½ teaspoons dried yeast or 12 g fresh
    yeast
200 ml tepid water
50 g rye flour
50 g wholemeal flour
300 g strong white flour
1 teaspoon salt

1. First make the starter. Put the yeast into a bowl and stir in the water. Leave to rest for 10 minutes. Sieve the flour and stir it into the water. Cover the bowl with a wet tea towel and leave it in the kitchen to ferment for a minimum of two days. Stir it two or three times a day. Refrigerate until needed.

2. To make the dough, put the yeast into a small bowl and stir in the water. Leave to rest for 5 minutes. Sieve the flours together into a mixing bowl and add the salt. Fix a dough hook attachment to your food mixer. Measure 250 ml of the starter and add this to the flour. Pour in the yeast and water and mix everything together on low speed for about 10 minutes.

3. If the mixture appears to be a little dry, add some more tepid water, a tablespoon at a time. Turn the dough out onto a lightly floured work surface and knead it for a further 10 minutes until it becomes smooth and elastic. Place in a lightly floured bowl, cover with a wet tea towel and leave it to rise for about 2 hours in a warm place.

4. Turn out the dough onto a lightly floured surface, knead it for a further 5 minutes, then leave to rest for about 10 minutes. Shape the dough into a ball or round loaf. Place on a floured baking tray, cover it again with a wet tea towel and leave to prove for 1½ hours until it has doubled in size.

5. Preheat the oven to 220°C/425°F/Gas 7. Place a baking tray in the oven to get hot.

6. Cut three parallel slashes about 5 mm deep across the top of the dough. Cut three more in the opposite direction to make a lattice pattern. Dust with a little flour, place on the hot tray and bake for 50 minutes or until golden brown. When cooked it should sound hollow when tapped. Leave it to cool on a rack.

Oggies

Since I have moved to Devon, I have noticed that all the pastry shops seem to sell pasties. The fillings vary and everyone here makes the point that Devon pasties are far better than those found in Cornwall. I suppose it should be no surprise to say that Cornish folk disagree with this and say that theirs are best! Everyone you meet has the best recipe. It is a bit like the mystique that surrounds the cassoulet in France. One thing is for sure, pasties or oggies (as the locals call them) are a complete meal. When I have been out shooting or fishing on a cold morning there is nothing I like better than coming home to a hot pasty and a pint of Otter. The best sauce accompaniment for oggies is HP, but I haven't got the recipe!

Serves 8

Pastry

375 g plain flour

15 g salt

125 g unsalted butter, cut into dice

125 g lard, cut into dice

1 egg, beaten

60 ml cold water

Filling

450 g topside of beef, cut into small
   pieces

1 onion, diced into 1-cm cubes

200 g potato, peeled and diced into
   1-cm cubes

1 carrot, peeled and diced into
   1-cm cubes

1 turnip, peeled and diced into
   1-cm cubes

salt and freshly milled black pepper

15 g parsley, chopped

1 teaspoon Worcestershire sauce

1 egg, beaten

1. Sieve the flour and salt into a large bowl. Add the butter and lard and rub them into the flour until the mixture resembles breadcrumbs. Add the beaten egg and pour in the water. Gently bind the pastry together and press it into a ball. Wrap in cling film and refrigerate for at least 2 hours.

2. Put the meat into a bowl. Add the onion, potato, carrot and turnip, stir together and season with salt and lots of pepper. Add the parsley and the Worcestershire sauce and stir everything together.

3. Cut the pastry in half and roll it out. Cut out eight circles about 16 cm in diameter. Brush around the edges of each circle with the beaten egg. Divide the filling into eight and spread it in a line across the centre of each circle of pastry. Fold the pastry over the filling so that the two sides meet. Using your thumb and forefinger, squeeze the pastry together to seal and crimp the edges. Brush the tops with the remaining egg wash and make small holes in the tops to allow the steam to escape.

4. Cook them in an oven preheated to 200°C/400°F/Gas 6 for about 25 minutes. Lower the oven temperature to 180°C/350°F/Gas 4 and cook for a further 25 minutes. Serve hot.

Naan Bread

Naan bread originates from the Punjat region in northern India. It is traditionally baked inside a very hot, dome-shaped clay oven called a tandoor.

**Makes 4 large breads,
enough for 8**

15 g fresh yeast
250 ml milk
500 g plain flour
1 teaspoon salt
1 teaspoon caster sugar
3 tablespoons natural live yoghurt
30 g ghee or unsalted melted butter

1. Crumble the yeast into a bowl and pour in the milk. Stir together with a whisk until the yeast has dissolved. Mix the flour and salt together in another bowl, then add the sugar, yoghurt and ghee. Pour in the milk and yeast liquid, stirring as you do so, to form a stiff, sticky dough.

2. Scrape out the dough onto a lightly floured work surface. Sprinkle a little more flour on top of the dough and knead it for at least 10 minutes until the dough becomes elastic. Transfer the dough to a clean bowl, cover with a wet tea towel and put somewhere warm (such as an airing cupboard) to prove for at least 4 hours until doubled in size.

3. Turn out the dough onto a lightly floured work surface and knock it back, kneading it for a further 5 minutes. Leave the dough to rest for 10 minutes, then cut it into four equal pieces. Sprinkle a little more flour onto the work surface, roll out each piece to form a rough circle 15 cm in diameter with a thickness of 6 mm, then take the dough in your hands and pull it apart to form an oval shape about 25 cm long.

4. Turn the grill on full and place a baking sheet underneath it to heat. This will take about 3 minutes. Place two of the naan breads at a time on the baking sheet and cook for about 3 minutes on each side or until they are golden in colour and slightly risen. Serve hot.

White Loaf

This is a simple recipe. The bread can be made in a loaf tin or divided into two and rolled into baguettes or French sticks. You could also cut it into eight equal-sized rolls.

25 g fresh yeast (or 3 teaspoons dried yeast)
380 ml luke warm water
525 g strong white bread flour
1 teaspoon salt

1. Sprinkle the yeast into a bowl and add 325 ml of luke warm water. Whisk until the yeast has fully dissolved, then leave to stand for 10 minutes.

2. Sift 150g of the flour into another bowl and add the salt. Make a well in the centre and pour in the liquid yeast. Stir the mixture together with a wooden spoon to form a smooth paste. Cover the bowl with a tea towel soaked in warm water and put somewhere warm (the airing cupboard is a good place) for about 30 minutes or until the dough has risen and become frothy.

3. Mix in the remaining flour and add the remaining water, a little at a time to form a soft, sticky dough. Put the wet cloth back over the bowl and leave it to rise in a warm place for about 1½ hours or until it has at least doubled its size.

4. Turn out the dough onto a lightly floured work surface and knead it for about 5 minutes or until it becomes firm and elastic. Put the dough back in the bowl to prove again for about 40 minutes, then repeat the process.

5. Preheat the oven to 230°C/450°F/Gas 8.

6. Decide which shape of bread you would like. For baguettes, cut the dough in half, then shape and roll them into 40-cm long sausages. Place them on a floured baking tray, cover with the tea towel and leave to prove for a further 45 minutes. The bread will double its size. With a sharp knife, cut several diagonal slashes across the top of the baguettes, then bake in the oven for 20–25 minutes. If making a loaf, you will need to bake it 40 minutes; if making rolls, 15–17 minutes. When the bread is cooked, it should be golden brown in colour and sound hollow when tapped underneath. Transfer it to a wire rack to cool before eating.

Caraway Biscuits

Serve these delicious biscuits with cheese.

Makes 30

175 g wholemeal flour

175 g plain flour

7 g crushed sea salt

50 g demerara sugar

150 g unsalted butter, cut into dice

50 ml cold water

1 egg, beaten until smooth

2 tablespoons caraway seeds

1. Sift the flours into a bowl, then add the salt and demerara sugar. Add the butter and rub it into the flour until the mixture resembles breadcrumbs. Stir the water into the beaten egg and pour this liquid into the flour. Knead the mixture to form a dough, then put in the refrigerator to rest for about 15 minutes.

2. Roll out the dough on a lightly floured surface to a thickness of 3 mm. Prick the dough all over with a fork. Sprinkle the dough with the caraway seeds and press them in gently using a rolling pin.

3. Preheat the oven to 230°C/450°F/Gas 8.

4. Lightly flour a baking tray. Using a plain 7.5-cm round cutter, cut out 30 biscuits, place them on the tray, then bake in the oven for about 15 minutes until golden.

Olive Oil Biscuits

Like Caraway Biscuits (see page 208), these are fantastic with cheese.

Makes about 80
300 g strong white bread flour
8 g salt
10 g fresh yeast
80 ml best virgin olive oil
100 ml warm water
ground semolina for dusting

1. Sift the flour into a large bowl. Add the salt and crumble the yeast into the flour. Gradually add the olive oil and warm water and mix the dough until it becomes smooth.

2. Place the dough onto a lightly floured worktop. Knead it for about 5 minutes and then put it back into the bowl. Cover the bowl with cling film and put it somewhere warm to prove for about 45 minutes – the airing cupboard is a good place.

3. Pre-heat the oven to 230°C/450°F/Gas 8. When the dough has proved, turn it out onto a floured surface and cut it into four equally sized pieces.

4. Roll out the dough into rectangles 2 mm thick and cut the biscuits to size. It is up to you how big you want them but I find that squares of 50 mm are a good size.

5. Sprinkle your baking sheets with a little flour and the ground semolina and lay out the biscuits in uniform lines almost touching each other. Repeat this process with the remaining dough.

6. Cook the biscuits for about 10 minutes or until they are a pale golden colour. Take them out and lay them on a rack to cool. Store in an airtight container. They keep for about five days this way.

Anchovy and Parmesan Straws

These are great served as pre-dinner nibbles with drinks.

Makes 30

120 g Puff Pastry (see page 213)
9 anchovy fillets
1 egg, beaten until smooth
30 g Parmesan cheese, grated
1 pinch cayenne pepper
1 teaspoon coarse sea salt

1. Cut the pastry in two and, on a lightly floured surface, roll out each half into a 20 x 15 cm rectangle. Place one rectangle of pastry on a piece of greaseproof paper. Lay three anchovy fillets in the middle, along the length of the pastry. Place another three anchovies approximately 3 cm above the middle strip, again along the length of the pastry. Place the remaining anchovies 3 cm below the middle strip of anchovies, again along the length of the pastry. Brush some of the beaten egg between the strips of anchovies. Carefully lay the other sheet of pastry on the top of the pastry with the anchovies and gently press the two sheets together. Place on a baking tray and put it in the freezer for about an hour to firm.

2. Preheat the oven to 230°C/450°F/Gas 8.

3. Remove the pastry from the freezer. Brush the top with more egg wash. Mix the Parmesan, cayenne pepper and sea salt together and sprinkle half of it over the egg wash. Turn the pastry over and again brush egg wash over the top. Sprinkle with the remaining Parmesan, cayenne pepper and salt. With a sharp knife, cut into 6-mm strips along the width of the pastry. Place the straws on a baking tray lined with greaseproof paper and cook in the oven for about 10 minutes or until golden brown.

Essentials

Puff Pastry

It is very important when making puff pastry to adequately chill it in between rollings. If you rush it, the butter will be too soft and will just pour out during cooking, with the result that the pastry will not rise properly. For good results, it is also important not to roll it out too thinly – it should never be less than a thickness of about 1 cm – and to cut the edges cleanly since pressed edges will not rise evenly.

Makes 1.25 kg
500 g plain flour
10 g salt
475 g unsalted butter
240 ml cold water
1 tablespoon lemon juice

1. Sieve the flour into a large bowl and add the salt. Dice 120 g of the butter into small cubes, then rub it into the flour until the mixture resembles breadcrumbs. Make a well in the centre of the flour, add the cold water and lemon juice, and mix to form a dough. Wrap the dough in cling film and leave it to rest in the refrigerator for at least 4 hours. The dough needs plenty of time to relax.
2. Take the dough from the refrigerator and place on a lightly floured work surface. With a knife, make a deep cross on the top. Then, working from the centre outwards, roll out the four corners to form a rough square. Make the corner 'flaps' thinner than the centre.
3. Put the remaining butter into a bowl and beat it to soften it but do not melt it – it should be soft enough to mould. Shape the butter to form a square and place it in the centre of the dough. Fold over each corner flap, completely enveloping the butter. Put the pastry in the refrigerator for at least 1 hour so that the dough and the butter cool to the same temperature.
4. Remove the pastry from the refrigerator and place on a lightly floured surface. Rolling away from you, roll out the dough to form a rectangle about 50 x 25 cm. Mentally divide the rectangle of pastry into three. Fold the bottom third up and over the middle third, then fold the top third down over both. Give the block a quarter turn from 12 o'clock to 3 o'clock, roll out again, and fold again into three. Press the edges lightly together and rest for 1 hour in the refrigerator.
5. Remove the pastry from the refrigerator and repeat the rolling out to a rectangle, folding, rolling, folding and chilling procedure twice more. The pastry needs a total of six three-fold turns. Return the pastry to the refrigerator for at least 2 hours before use.

Shortcrust Pastry

Makes 700 g
375 g plain flour
15 g salt
225 g unsalted butter, cut into dice
1 egg
60 ml cold water

1. Sieve the flour and salt into a bowl, add the butter and rub it into the flour until the mixture resembles coarse breadcrumbs.
2. Beat the egg with a fork in a small bowl until smooth.
3. Make a well in the centre of the flour. Add the beaten egg and the cold water and gently bind everything together until thoroughly mixed, then press into a ball. Wrap the pastry in cling film and refrigerate until needed.

Sweet Pastry

Makes about 1 kg
300 g unsalted butter
110 g icing sugar
2 eggs
500 g soft plain flour

1. Beat the butter and icing sugar together until light and fluffy. Add the eggs, one at a time, and beat into the butter until smooth. Add the flour and mix to a smooth paste that comes away cleanly from the sides of the bowl.
2. Turn out the pastry onto a lightly floured surface and mould it to form a ball. Cover in cling film and place in the refrigerator to rest for at least 2 hours before using.

Chicken Stock

This is the stock that I use the most – not just for chicken cookery, but as a base to all bird dishes. I also use it for some veal and fish cookery, and in certain vegetable and potato dishes. It has the most delicate of flavours and is the one that is the most rounded as a base to sauce cookery. I probably could not function without it! Make a large amount and store in smaller airtight containers in your freezer until needed.

Makes 3 litres
2 kg chicken bones (you can use chicken carcasses or chicken winglets)
4 litres water

1 large onion, cut in half
1 carrot, roughly chopped
1 leek, roughly chopped
2 celery sticks, roughly chopped
4 garlic cloves, peeled
1 teaspoon cracked white peppercorns
1 sprig fresh thyme
1 bay leaf
handful of parsley stalks

1. Put the chicken bones into a large stockpot, add the water and put on the stove to boil. With a ladle, remove all the surfacing sediment and discard. Lower the heat to a simmer.

2. Add the onion, carrot, leek and celery to the simmering stock, along with the garlic, peppercorns, thyme, bay leaf and parsley. Bring the stock back to the boil, skim off the surfacing foam and discard. Lower the heat and simmer for a minimum of 3½ hours.

3. Strain the stock through a fine sieve and allow to cool before refrigerating or freezing.

Fish Stock

The best bones for fish stock are from flat fish such as sole, turbot, brill or halibut. They need to be what are called 'white fish bones'. Do not use any dark skin from the fish when making this, as it will affect the colour of the stock. It will keep in the refrigerator for up to three to four days. Noilly Prat is perfect for this stock as it is a fruity vermouth; most other ordinary vermouths are too bitter.

Makes 1.5 litres
2 kg fish bones (trimmed and washed)
60 ml olive oil
60 g unsalted butter
3 onions, sliced
3 garlic cloves, peeled and chopped
1 large sprig fresh thyme
handful of parsley stalks
½ teaspoon dried fennel seeds
350 ml Noilly Prat
750 ml dry white wine
1.5 litres water

1. Preheat the oven to 180°C/350°F/Gas 4.
2. Wash the bones, trim off any dark fins and skin and discard, then chop and put to one side. Make sure that any gills left in the fish heads are cut out.

3. Heat the olive oil in a large lidded saucepan that can subsequently go in the oven and add the butter. Add the onions and garlic and stir for 2–3 minutes. Do not colour the onions. Add the thyme, parsley stalks and fennel seeds. Pour in the Noilly Prat, then bring to the boil. Continue to boil until the liquid has been reduced by at least half and has started to become syrupy.

4. Add the white wine, return to the boil, and reduce the liquid by half. Add the water. Bring the stock back to the boil and, with a ladle, skim off all the surfacing sediment and discard. Carefully add the fish bones and once again return to the boil. Skim off all the surfacing sediment and discard. The water should just cover the bones. Cover the pan with greaseproof paper and the lid, then place in the oven for 15 minutes.

5. Remove the pan from the oven, take off the lid and paper and pour the contents of the pan into a colander set over a large bowl. Discard the bones. Strain the stock through a muslin cloth into plastic containers and allow to cool. When cold, seal with airtight lids and freeze until needed.

Lamb Stock

As with all the stocks in this book, you can freeze any that you do not use on the day in airtight containers. Ask your butcher to chop the bones into small pieces for you – the best bones to use are the ones that are taken from shinning the best ends.

Makes 1 litre
1 kg lamb bones, chopped small
2 tablespoons olive oil
2 onions, cut in half
1 carrot, peeled and roughly chopped
1 celery stick, roughly chopped
1 leek, roughly chopped
3 garlic cloves
1 sprig thyme
1 bay leaf
1 tablespoon tomato purée
3 tomatoes, cut in half and deseeded
1 litre water
salt
1 teaspoon crushed black peppercorns

1. Preheat the oven to 200°C/400°F/Gas 6.
2. Place the bones in a roasting tray and sprinkle them with a little cold water. Put them in the oven to brown. This will take about 30 minutes.

3. Place a large saucepan or stockpot on the stove to heat. Add the olive oil, then the onions, and fry until browned. Put all the vegetables in the pan and brown them too. Peel and crush the garlic and add to the pan, along with the thyme and bay leaf. Stir in the tomato purée and the tomatoes. Pour in the water and season with a little salt and the crushed black peppercorns.

4. Remove the bones from the oven and strain them through a colander set over a bowl to trap the fat. Add the bones into the stock and bring the liquid to the boil as quickly as possible. With a ladle, skin off all the surfacing sediment and discard. Lower the heat, and cook at a moderate simmer for 3 hours.

5. Strain the stock first through a colander set over a large bowl, then through a fine sieve or muslin cloth into plastic containers and allow to cool. When cold, seal with airtight lids and freeze until needed.

Beef/Veal Stock

This stock can be used as the base to all the veal and beef dishes in this book. This recipe makes 4 litres of finished stock; reduced it will make 1.5 litres of gravy. For certain dishes, it might be necessary to reduce the stock by half or more to achieve the correct flavour or thickness for the sauce. For gravies, the stock can be thickened with a little diluted cornflour or flour.

Makes 4 litres
2.5 kg beef bones, chopped small
1 kg veal shank or similar cheap cut, cut in half
1 tablespoon vegetable oil
500 g large ripe tomatoes, cut in half and deseeded
2 garlic cloves, peeled
4 onions, roughly chopped
2 carrots, peeled and roughly chopped
2 sticks celery, roughly chopped
2 leeks, roughly chopped
4 parsley stalks
1 bay leaf
1 sprig thyme
1 teaspoon crushed white peppercorns
1 teaspoon salt
300 g mushrooms, sliced
1.5 litres water

1. Preheat the oven to 200°C/400°F/Gas 6.
2. Put the beef bones in a roasting tray, sprinkle a little water over them, then roast them in the oven until they are dark brown. This will take about 30 minutes.

3. Heat a little vegetable oil in a large saucepan. As soon as the oil starts to smoke, lay the two pieces of veal shank in the oil and cook them until they are coloured on both sides. Remove the veal and put into a large stockpot. Remove the beef bones from the oven and strain them into a colander set over a bowl to trap the fat. Spoon the beef bones over the veal.

4. Add the tomatoes and garlic to the stockpot, along with the onions, carrots, celery, leeks, herbs, peppercorns and salt. Put the mushrooms on top, add the water, and put the stockpot on the stove to boil. As the stock begins to boil, a great deal of fat and froth will surface. With a ladle, remove and discard. It is important to do this or you will end up with a cloudy unpleasant result. Lower the heat, and simmer for a minimum of 8 hours, skimming periodically.

5. Strain the stock first through a colander into a large saucepan and then through a fine sieve into plastic containers and allow to cool. When cold, seal with airtight lids and freeze until needed.

Court Bouillon or Poaching Stock

Court bouillon can be used to poach all shellfish, including crab, lobster and langoustines. It can also be used to poach fish such as salmon and turbot.

Makes 2 litres
1 large onion, cut into 1-cm dice
1 large carrot, peeled and diced
1 stick celery, chopped
½ bulb fennel, chopped
4 garlic cloves, peeled
60 ml olive oil
60 g parsley stalks
2 star anise
1 teaspoon fennel seeds
1 teaspoon crushed black peppercorns
60 ml white wine vinegar
120 ml dry white wine
2 litres water
30 g salt
juice of 1 lemon

1. Put the onion, carrot, celery, fennel and garlic into a large saucepan. Pour in the olive oil and put the pan on the stove over a high heat. Stir and cook the vegetables for about 5 minutes.

215

2. Add the parsley stalks, star anise, fennel seeds and crushed peppercorns. Pour in the white wine vinegar and reduce it to syrup. Add the white wine and boil it until its volume has been reduced by half. Add the water and return the stock to the boil. With a ladle, skim off all the surfacing sediment and discard. Lower the heat and simmer for a further 10 minutes. Add the salt and lemon juice.

3. Bring the stock back to the boil when you are ready to poach the shellfish or fish.

Vegetable Stock

This will keep in the refrigerator for a week.

Makes 2 litres

1 onion
1 large carrot
2 sticks celery
250 g white button mushrooms
1 leek
2 turnips
1 swede
1 celeriac bulb
2 litres water
2 sprigs flat-leaf parsley
1 small bunch chervil
1 sprig thyme
1 bay leaf
salt and freshly milled black pepper

1. Wash, peel and chop all the vegetables, then place them in a large lidded saucepan and cover with the water. Add the herbs, season with salt and pepper, and bring to the boil on the stove. As it comes up to the boil, sediment will rise to the surface. Remove this with a ladle and discard.

2. Lower the heat to a light simmer, cover and cook gently for 30 minutes. Remove the pan from the heat, transfer the stock to a bowl and allow to cool.

3. Strain the vegetables through a colander and then through a muslin cloth to trap any sediment. Store in the refrigerator in an airtight container until required.

Butter Sauce

Enormously versatile, you can add mustard, dill, tomato dice, chervil, chives or parsley to butter sauce, to name but a few. It is mostly used for fish, but you can also use it with steamed vegetables and potatoes.

Makes about 300 ml

2 shallots or 1 onion, finely chopped
1 sprig fresh tarragon
1 garlic clove, chopped
1 sprig fresh thyme
½ bay leaf
½ teaspoon crushed white peppercorns
250 g unsalted butter
30 ml white wine vinegar
30 ml white wine
30 ml double cream
salt
lemon juice to taste

1. Put the shallots in a small saucepan with the tarragon. Add the garlic, along with the thyme, bay leaf and crushed peppercorns. Cut off about 20 g of butter and add to the rest of the ingredients. Put the pan on the stove and melt the butter, stirring as you do so.

2. Add the white wine vinegar and boil until it has been reduced to a syrup. Add the white wine and do the same.

3. Cut the remaining butter into small pieces. Pour the double cream into the pan and, as soon as it boils, lower the heat. Add the butter, piece by piece, stirring until it is all melted and you have a smooth sauce. Add some salt and squeeze in a little lemon juice.

4. Pour the finished sauce through a fine sieve into another small pan. Keep warm.

White Sauce

This can be used as a base for several cream sauces, or, diluted with cream, it can be used as a sauce on its own for broad beans, cauliflower cheese, etc. It is also a good thickening agent – I use it for just this purpose in my Onion Tart recipe (see page 141). With the addition of breadcrumbs and cream, it can also be used as a bread sauce to accompany roast chicken.

Makes 300 ml

1 small onion
1 clove
450 ml milk
¼ bay leaf
a pinch of grated nutmeg
60 g unsalted butter
60 g plain flour

1. Peel the onion and stud it with the clove. Pour the milk into a saucepan, add the onion and bay leaf, grate in a little nutmeg, and bring to the boil. When the milk has boiled, lower the heat to a simmer.

2. Melt the butter in another saucepan and stir in the flour using a wooden spoon. When thoroughly mixed, but before the flour takes any colour, gradually strain in the milk. Do this a little at a time so the sauce doesn't go lumpy. Stir the sauce until smooth, then allow it to cook out for about 30 minutes over a very low heat.

3. Pour the sauce through a conical strainer into a bowl, pushing it through with a spatula. Put a small knob of butter on top of the sauce to prevent a skin forming.

Tartare Sauce

This is the perfect accompaniment to Haddock in Batter (see page 50).

Makes 350 ml
300 ml Mayonnaise (see page 218)
25 g gherkins, finely chopped
25 g capers, finely chopped
25 g chervil, chopped
25 g shallots, chopped
25 g parsley, chopped
lemon juice
salt
1 pinch cayenne pepper, to taste

Pour the mayonnaise into a bowl, then stir in the gherkins and capers. Add the chervil, shallots and parsley. Season with a little lemon juice, some salt and a pinch of cayenne pepper.

Horseradish Sauce

An essential accompaniment to roast beef, and good, too, with smoked salmon or smoked trout. It will keep in the refrigerator for about 1 week.

Makes 250 ml
60 g horseradish, peeled and finely grated
1 teaspoon Dijon mustard
juice of ½ lemon
1½ teaspoons caster sugar
salt and freshly milled black pepper
2 tablespoons Mayonnaise (see page 218)
150 ml double cream

1. Place the horseradish in a bowl. Stir in the mustard and lemon juice. Add the caster sugar and season

with a little salt and pepper. Stir in the mayonnaise.

2. Pour the cream into another bowl and whisk it to a soft peak. Carefully fold it into the horseradish and gently mix together. Refrigerate until needed.

Cumberland Sauce

This is an excellent accompaniment to a variety of cold meats and game terrines, for example Wild Duck Terrine with Pistachio Nuts (see pages 84–5). It should keep for at least a week in the refrigerator.

Serves 8
1 orange
1 shallot, finely chopped
juice of ½ lemon
150 ml ruby port
½ teaspoon ground mixed spice
1 teaspoon root ginger, finely chopped
350 g redcurrant jelly

1. Peel the zest from the orange. With a sharp knife, cut away any pith on the zest and discard (this is bitter and must be removed). Cut the zest into long, very fine strips, then put in a small saucepan. Cut the orange half and squeeze the juice over the zest through a fine sieve.

2. Add the shallot to the orange. Add the lemon juice, squeezing it through another fine sieve. Pour in the port and add the ground spice and root ginger.

3. Put the pan on the stove over a medium heat and boil the liquid until it has been reduced to a third of its original volume. This will take about 15 minutes.

4. Remove the pan from heat and stir in the redcurrant jelly. Mix well. Pour the sauce into an airtight preserving jar and allow to cool. Close the lid and refrigerate until needed.

Hollandaise Sauce

This sauce is the base to countless compound sauces. For Bearnaise, for example, just add herbs. The sauce must always be served warm.

Serves 4
25 g unsalted butter
1 shallot, finely chopped
1 garlic clove, peeled and finely chopped
½ teaspoon crushed black peppercorns
1 sprig fresh tarragon
1 sprig fresh thyme
½ bay leaf

1 parsley stalk
25 ml white wine vinegar
25 ml dry white wine
2 egg yolks
1 dessertspoon cold water
75 ml Clarified Butter (see below)
salt
1 pinch cayenne pepper
juice of ½ lemon

1. Melt the butter in a saucepan, then add the shallots, garlic, peppercorns and herbs. Cook over a moderate heat for about 5 minutes but do not allow the ingredients to colour.
2. Pour the vinegar into the pan and boil until it has totally evaporated. Add the wine and again boil the liquid until it has been reduced to a syrup. Take the pan off the heat, remove the herbs and discard.
3. Place a saucepan of water on the stove to boil. Put the egg yolks in a stainless steel bowl, add the cold water, and place the bowl over the saucepan, which should be just below boiling point. Whisk the yolks until they thicken and form soft peaks.
4. Gradually add the warm clarified butter, whisking rapidly all the time until the sauce becomes smooth. Add the wine and shallot reduction, and continue beating vigorously over the hot water. Season the sauce with a little salt and a pinch of cayenne pepper. Squeeze in the lemon juice. Serve.

Mayonnaise

This makes a delicious accompaniment to many dishes as well as forming the basis of dozens of cold sauces. Stored in an airtight container in the refrigerator, it will keep for several days.

Makes 300 ml
3 small egg yolks
1 teaspoon warm water
25 g Dijon mustard
60 ml malt vinegar
25 g caster sugar
150 ml olive oil
150 ml vegetable oil
salt
cayenne pepper
lemon juice

1. Put the egg yolks in a stainless steel bowl. Add the warm water and the mustard and whisk together.
2. Pour the vinegar into a small pan, add the sugar and, over a high heat, melt the sugar. Reduce the vinegar until it becomes syrupy. Remove the pan from the heat and allow to cool.
3. Mix the two oils together in a jug and, very slowly, start pouring the oil into the egg yolks, whisking all the time. It is important that the oils are not too cold or the mayonnaise will curdle. When half of the oil is incorporated into the egg yolks, thin the mayonnaise by adding the vinegar. Continue pouring in the oil, mixing continuously until smooth. Season with salt and cayenne pepper and squeeze in a few drops of lemon juice.

Garlic Tomato Mayonnaise

The French call this rouille. Traditionally, it was made by using crushed and dried shellfish carcasses such as crab and lobster – the shells were ground to a powder to thicken and flavour the sauce. This is a more modern recipe, but delicious nonetheless.

Makes 200 ml
2 teaspoons cayenne pepper
5 garlic cloves, peeled
2 egg yolks
salt
125 ml olive oil
4 teaspoons tomato purée
lemon juice

1. Place the cayenne pepper, garlic cloves, egg yolks and a little salt in a mortar and pound them to a smooth paste.
2. Put the paste into a large stainless steel bowl and, with a whisk, beat in the olive oil, a little at a time. The eggs should thicken and become creamy. Be careful not to add the oil too quickly or the sauce will curdle. If the sauce becomes too thick, just add a teaspoonful of warm water to loosen it.
3. Stir in the tomato purée. Season with a little more salt to taste, and add a squeeze of lemon juice.

Clarified Butter

Makes 200 ml
350 g unsalted butter, cut into small pieces

1. Put the butter in a small saucepan and melt it over a very gentle heat. As the butter melts, all the curds, whey and impurities will rise to the surface. Using a small ladle, skim these off and discard. There will be some milk underneath the butter.

2. Carefully pour the clarified butter into a bowl through a sieve lined with muslin to trap all the impurities. Stop pouring when you reach the milk. Put to one side until needed.

A Basic Pasta Dough

I know it's easy to just buy ready-made or dried pasta but, like bread, the difference between bought and home-made is amazing. It's really very simple to make, and the pasta machine needed to roll and cut it is not expensive. Wrapped in cling film, it will keep in the fridge for up to three days.

Makes 500 g
4 whole eggs
5 egg yolks
500 g strong white bread flour, sieved
½ teaspoon salt
1 teaspoon good olive oil

1. Crack the whole eggs into a bowl, then add the yolks. Beat them together with a whisk until smooth.
2. Put the flour and salt into the bowl of a Kenwood Chef or similar machine. Set the machine at its lowest speed and gradually add the beaten eggs and egg yolks. Mix to a smooth paste. Pour the olive oil into the bowl. Increase the speed, and beat for about 2 minutes to form a smooth dough.
3. Remove the pasta dough from the machine, wrap it in cling film so that it is airtight, and allow to relax for at least 20 minutes before use. If you attempt to roll it immediately, it will be too elastic and tough.
4. Either roll the pasta through a machine or roll it out by hand on a lightly floured work surface using a rolling pin. Roll it out as thinly as possible, then cut into the shape required: into long thin strips for fettuccine or tagliatelle, wider strips for pappardelle, or broad rectangles for lasagne.
5. It can either be cooked immediately, for 1 or 2 minutes only in boiling salted water, or left to dry a little. Dried home-made pasta will take a few minutes longer to cook.

Walnut Oil Vinaigrette

This keeps for at least a couple of weeks in a cool place.

Serves 6–8
18 ml sherry vinegar
1 teaspoon lemon juice
150 ml groundnut oil
150 ml walnut oil
1 small garlic clove, peeled and crushed
1 pinch sugar
1 pinch salt and freshly ground black pepper

Pour all the ingredients into a bowl and whisk together. Pour the vinaigrette through a funnel into a small bottle fitted with a cork or into an airtight jar. Remember to shake the vinaigrette well before using.

Variation
For hazelnut vinaigrette, substitute a hazelnut oil for the walnut one.

Tarragon Vinaigrette

This dressing works well with most lettuces, especially the lighter coloured ones such as little gem, frisée, chicory and iceberg – add a little finely chopped shallots and chives to the salad to enhance the flavour. It will keep for more than a week in the refrigerator.

Makes 630 ml
2 garlic cloves
juice of ½ lemon
120 ml white wine vinegar
salt and freshly milled black pepper
a pinch of caster sugar
500 ml olive oil
3 sprigs fresh tarragon

1. Peel the garlic cloves, cut in half, and set aside.
2. Put the lemon juice, wine vinegar, salt and pepper and sugar in a bowl. Whisk in the olive oil, then, using a small funnel, pour into a jar or bottle, and add the garlic cloves and sprigs of tarragon. Put a lid or cork on the bottle or jar. Shake well before using.

Custard

Only the vanilla seeds are used here; the pods can be saved and used to flavour sugar, which is great for cake baking. The custard will keep for up to three days in the refrigerator in a sealed container.

Serves 6–8
500 ml milk
2 vanilla pods
6 egg yolks
100 g caster sugar

1. Pour the milk into a saucepan. Split the vanilla pods in half lengthways, scrape out the seeds with the point of a sharp knife, and add them to the milk. Gently heat the milk and, as soon as it reaches boiling point, take it off the stove. Put to one side.
2. Whisk together the egg yolks and caster sugar until they become pale in colour. Pour half the milk into the eggs and sugar, whisking as you do so, and continue to whisk until smooth. Pour back into the milk in the saucepan.
3. Put the saucepan back on the stove and, over a moderate heat, stir the custard until it has thickened enough to coat the back of a spoon. Continue stirring but *do not boil* – if you do, the eggs will scramble and the custard will be ruined. Pour the custard into a bowl until it is required.

Pastry Cream

Pastry cream can be used in a multitude of ways – as a base to a soufflé, mixed with whipped cream to fill eclairs or choux buns, or set as a vanilla mousse. It will keep for up to three days in the refrigerator.

Makes 800 g
600 ml milk
1 vanilla pod
30 g cornflour
30 g plain flour
6 egg yolks
120 g caster sugar

1. Pour the milk into a saucepan. Cut the vanilla pod in two, lengthways, and, using the point of a sharp knife, scrape out the seeds. Put both the pod and the seeds into the milk and bring to the boil.
2. Meanwhile, mix together the two flours. Whisk the egg yolks with the sugar in a bowl until pale in colour and beginning thicken. Add the flour and whisk

together thoroughly. Pour about a third of the boiling milk over the egg, sugar and flour and mix together until smooth. Pour the mixture into the milk in the saucepan. Bring back to the boil, whisking all the time.
3. When it has boiled and thickened, transfer the cream to a bowl, cover with cling film and, when cold, refrigerate.

Stock Syrup

This syrup can be used to poach fruits such as apples, pears, peaches, etc. It is also used to make sorbets, and is added to numerous egg-based sabayon dishes. It will keep for up to 2 weeks.

Makes about 1 litre
500 ml water
650 g caster sugar
juice of 1 lemon

1. Pour the water into a large saucepan and add the sugar. Squeeze the lemon juice into the pan and bring to the boil on the stove. As soon as it has boiled and the sugar has dissolved, turn off the heat and allow to cool.
2. When cold, pour into an airtight container.

Index

For Kim

To the ratbags Eve, Olivia, Martha-Daisy, Eliza, Charles, Amelia, Fendi and Basil; to my mum.

To all the people that helped me with this project:
Pat Llewellyn, Series Executive Producer (the boss!)
Everyone at Optomen Television, the best crew in the world,
led by Paul Ratcliffe, Series Producer/Director (you know!);
Emma Bowen, Edit Producer; Lesley Gardner, Head of
Production; Gail Pinkerton, Production Manager; Jennie
Macdiarmid, Assistant Producer; Catrin Darnell, Researcher;
Richard Hill, Camera; Rex Phillips, Sound Recordist; Jeremy
Cracknell, Location & Camera Assistant; Mike Sarah,
Lighting; Daniel Pemberton, Music; Philippa Daniel, Editor;
Jon Hubbard, Editor; Michael Pipkin, Assistant Editor.
At Channel 4: Mark Thompson, Emma Westcott, Daniella
Eversby and Sue Murphy.
To Michelle Brachet for all her work, help and support.
Fiona MacIntyre, Carey Smith, David Eldridge, Sarah Bennie,
Ros Ellis and the fantastic team at Ebury Press.
Nigel Marriage and Robin Zavou my head chefs, Jean
Bertrand de March, Emilie Poyet and Kathy Broussart.
Pia Tryde for all her inspirational photography and Jon
Ongkiehong her assistant. Caroline Marson (food stylist).
Miren Lopategui. Bo and Elaine at Robert Montgomery &
Partners. Special thanks to: Richard Halliday and Ken Giles,
Dartington Crystal. John Jackson, Royal Doulton. Steve
Loughton, Enodis. Patsy Narine, Geoff Pearson, Molly Ibbett
and Johnny Narine. Lionel Deyong, my intrepid accountant
and friend. All of the staff at The New Angel Restaurant.
Philip Narine and The New Angel builders. Eamonn O'Nolan.
Tom and Sally Jaine. Basil H. Williams, Chairman of the
Regatta. Councillor Richard Rendle MBE, Dartmouth Town
Mayor. Dartmouth Town Council. South Hams District
Council. Kingsbridge Community College. Kingsbridge
Community Primary School. Suzie Ward. Pauline & Derek
Adams, The Waterfront Coffee House. Suzie & Gabriel David,
Luscombe Organic Drinks. Mark Sharman, Sharpham
Partnership. Bob & Sue Ward, and Elliot Douglas, A.W.
Luscombe Butchers. Richard & Lesley Goodman, Gara Barton
Farm. David Edwards and Richard Ensor, Widfall Farm. Steve
Parker, Dave Drake, The Two Rivers Charter Boat. Dartmouth
Angling Club. Butlins Bognor Regis. Mike Humphries,
Barclays Bank. Graham Massey at GS Group. Simon Benson.
Sarah Storrs. Nick & Sally Hurst. Jim at the floating bridge.
The traffic warden in Dartmouth! Tom Brooks, Old Cummings
Farm. Justin Weeks, Sea Bass fisherman. Sarie Cooper,
Ticklemore Cheese. Nick Henry, Moby Nicks Fishmonger.
Carl Griffiths, lobster fisherman. Paul & Sally Vincent, eggs.
Robert Bruckner, dairy products. Paul Evans, fruit and
vegetables. Tony Quick, speciality produce. Mark Durrans,
crab fisherman. Sid Griffiths, bass fisherman.

Editorial Consultant: Miren Lopategui; Editor: Judith Hannam; Design: Two Associates; Photographer: Pia Tryde; Props Stylist:
Tessa Evelegh; Home economist: Caroline Marson; Indexer: Phyllis van Reenen. The publishers would also like to thank Sally
Vincent at Brambletorre for help with photography, and The Little Admiral Hotel in Dartmouth.
Pure wool rugs from Melin Tregwynt: 01348 891644, www.melintregwynt.co.uk
Fresh and pretty printed cotton tablecloths, napkins and aprons; large enamel jug, all from
Cath Kidston: 020 7229 8000, www.cathkidston.co.uk
Tableware supplied by Royal Doulton: www.royaldoulton.com

First published by Ebury Press, Random House, 20 Vauxhall Bridge Road, London SW1V 2SA
Random House Australia (Pty) Limited, 20 Alfred Street, Milsons Point, Sydney, New South Wales 2061, Australia
Random House New Zealand Limited, 18 Poland Road, Glenfield, Auckland 10, New Zealand
Random House South Africa (Pty) Limited, Endulini, 5A Jubilee Road, Parktown 2193, South Africa
The Random House Group Limited Reg. No. 954009
www.randomhouse.co.uk
A CIP catalogue record for this book is available from the British Library. ISBN 0091901634. Papers used by Ebury Press are
natural recyclable products made from wood grown in sustainable forests. Printed and bound by C&C Offset Printing Company
Limited in Hong Kong.